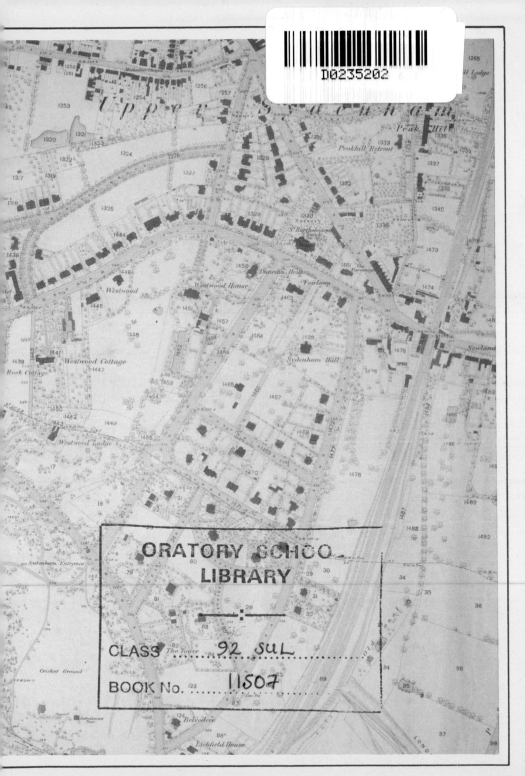

1863

Sullivan and the Scott Russells

Sullivan in the 1860s

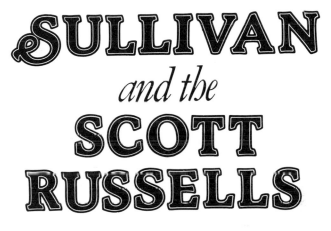

SULLIVAN
and the
SCOTT RUSSELLS

*A Victorian love affair
told through the letters of
Rachel and Louise Scott Russell
to Arthur Sullivan
1864-1870*

John Wolfson

A HEADLION BOOK
PACKARD PUBLISHING LIMITED
CHICHESTER

A Headlion book, first published in 1984 by
Packard Publishing Limited, 16 Lynch Down, Funtington,
Chichester, West Sussex PO18 9LR.

British Library Cataloguing in Publication Data
Wolfson, John
    Sullivan and the Scott Russells.
    1. Sullivan, *Sir* Arthur   2. Scott Russell,
    Louise   3. Scott Russell, Rachel
    4. Composers——Great Britain——Biography
    I. Title
    780'.92'2   ML410.S95

    ISBN 0-906527-14-7

Layout by Janet Kershaw based upon designs by Paul Sharp
Typeset in IBM Baskerville by Pauline Newton, Chichester
Printed in the United Kingdom by Olivers Printing Works Limited, Battle

Come to me my darling, I hold out my arms to you. Oh, come to them and let me forget the world and all its griefs in your great love. — May 1867

I put my hands in yours and looking straight into your clear dear eyes, I say, True unto death Arthur . . . now that a cloud has come over our sun. — July 1867

I spoke to Mama tonight, or rather she spoke to me . . . I cannot tell you all that passed, but her decisive words were, "I will sooner die than let you marry him . . ." — July 1867

Oh, darling, darling, I can scarcely bear the pain of this separation and the longing feelings I get and the loneliness and the fear that perhaps my darling may change. — August 1867

. . . dearest, I am speaking to you very earnestly now — sitting at your knees — with your dear hand against my cheek. Darling, our future lies more with you than with me . . . — December 1867

I have lost my youth. You are the only hope of bringing it back. Marry me. — January 1868

But for that meeting . . . I should never have feared. But I saw something in you so strongly developed that day — something which always frightens me which I dread. — April 1868

Oh darling, darling — don't let your beautiful love cool . . . if the heart gets cold the dove dies — and your life will never be the same. — July 1868

Oh darling, in the watches of the night those words of yours come back to me ringing in all their bitterness in my ears: "How shall I tell you when I do not love you?" Why did you say them? — July 1868

When you see this ring you will know that what I write now is to say "<u>Goodbye</u>". I should have written this when you left, but my courage failed . . . — February 1869

I have torn out my heart and sent it back to you but I quiver from head to foot in every fibre with the pain . . . My God how we have paid for every moment of happiness. — February 1869

I know you have told me not to write to you, but don't be angry. I sometimes feel as if my heart would break if I did not speak to you. — Spring 1869

The beginning of winter is always sad and it brings back to me those bright days when you came in the afternoon and we sat round the fire and had our tea and we chatted such nonsense. — December 1869

I am coming to spend the afternoon with you on Friday to burn my letters. — December 1869

I do not think that I shall ever love again. — January 1870

Contents

People Mentioned in the Letters

John Scott Russell (*Papa*) — 1808-1882
Harriette Scott Russell (*Mama*) — 1808-1888
Louise Scott Russell (*Lady*) — 1841-1878
Norman Scott Russell — 1843-*
Rachel Scott Russell (*Chennie*) — 1845-1882
Alice Scott Russell (*Dickie*) — 1847-1936

Frederick Clay — engaged to Alice, 1867-68
Harry Wynne — suitor to Rachel, Summer 1867
Arthur Sullivan — engaged to Rachel, 1867-68
Mr. Baxter — engaged to Alice, December 1868
François Rausch — married to Alice, September 1869
William Henn Holmes — married to Rachel, October 1872

* Norman Scott Russell was alive as late as 1925

List of Illustrations

Foreword

The correspondence between Rachel and Louise Scott Russell and Arthur Sullivan began in 1864 and ended in 1870. After that there was practically no contact between Sullivan and the Scott Russell family. Nonetheless, Sullivan kept the girls' letters all his life.

Herbert Sullivan, the composer's nephew, inherited the love letters with the bulk of his uncle's estate in 1900. For half a century no-one was permitted to see the letters, and hardly anyone knew of their existence. In 1924 Henry Saxe Wyndham requested permission to refer to Sullivan's relationship with Rachel in a biography of the composer which he was then writing. Saxe Wyndham, however, was not permitted to see the love letters, and in the end, was constrained to limit his mention of Rachel to a single paragraph. Three years later Herbert Sullivan published his own biography of his uncle and made no mention of Rachel at all.

Leslie Baily, author of *The Gilbert and Sullivan Book*, published in 1952, was permitted to read some of the love letters, which by then had become the property of Herbert Sullivan's widow. While Baily did quote from a few of the letters in this book he gave little indication of the real nature of Sullivan's relationship with the Scott Russells.

In 1964 the love letters were acquired with the Sullivan Archive by the Pierpont Morgan Library which has given permission for the letters to be quoted here.

There are approximately two hundred letters in the collection. About one hundred and fifty extracts are printed in the pages that follow, representing the most important part of the correspondence.

Rachel and Louise dated very few of their letters. Many of them, however, remain with their original envelopes whose postmarks have been used to establish some degree of chronology. The dates of all letters so identified have been listed, together with the sources of all other quotations used in this book, in a table beginning on page 125.

The letters, some of which are almost illegible, were frequently written in the heat of passion, and in great haste. They were punctuated with many dashes, underlinings and exclamation marks. These have been retained, except where the meaning of a sentence would be unclear unless the punctuation were altered. The ampersand has been expanded, but no further changes have been made.

Acknowledgements

This book would not have been possible without the use of materials in the Sullivan Archive at the Pierpont Morgan Library in New York City. I am grateful to Reginald Allen, former Curator of that collection, for the trust he showed in me by placing the entire Scott Russell correspondence at my disposal.

I am indebted to Professor Jane W. Stedman of Roosevelt University, Chicago, who read my manuscript and gave me much information on Victorian family life. I would like to acknowledge the comments of Professor George S. Emmerson of the University of Western Ontario, author of a book on Rachel's father. I owe thanks as well to Gladys Farrow Smith for providing me with many insights into the mysteries of Rachel's character.

Finally, I must give special acknowledgement to my friend I. de Keyser for his constant encouragement.

J.W.

CHAPTER ONE

The Three Sisters

(1863–May 1867)

I am a little frightened sometimes at the strength of the love that I have awakened in you.

— Rachel to Sullivan

The exterior of the Crystal Palace, Sydenham. Contemporary print

"So you see, it was good-bye after all", Louise Scott Russell wrote to Arthur Sullivan in December 1868.

Less than two months later, her younger sister, Rachel, wrote to Arthur Sullivan, "When you see this ring — you will know that what I write to say now is 'Goodbye'."

Two sisters, both in love with the same man, both renounced him in the same way at the same time, and both continued to mourn the loss of him for a long time thereafter. This curious story began and ended during the 1860s in the London suburb of Sydenham, in the shadow of the Crystal Palace.

Rachel and Louise Scott Russell had grown up not far from the Palace, which was a giant exhibition hall enclosed in steel and glass. As a young composer Arthur Sullivan had had his first orchestral works presented at the Crystal Palace in 1862, and Rachel and Louise had been going to the Saturday concerts there since 1855. It was music that brought the three of them together and it was music that would be the dominating force in their lives. Rachel once wrote to Sullivan:

> *Oh! darling, I am so glad you and music are one with me — but it is very painful to me sometimes. I cannot bear to hear a note of your music when you are not there — and oh! I do rejoice to sit by you again at those coming winter concerts and feel the chord of harmonized sympathy that knits us together, my love!*

Rachel and her parents had moved to Sydenham in 1852. Her father, John Scott Russell, was the son of a Scottish minister. Her Mother, Harriette, was a strong minded Irishwoman, and the daughter of Sir Daniel Toler Osborne, twelfth Baronet of Tipperary. The Scott Russells were married in 1838.

> *When my mother and father first came to London they were so poor that they lived in two tiny rooms in Westminster, and these were so filled with books they could scarcely find room to sit down and they were so poor that Mama could only go out after dark because her clothes were not nice.*

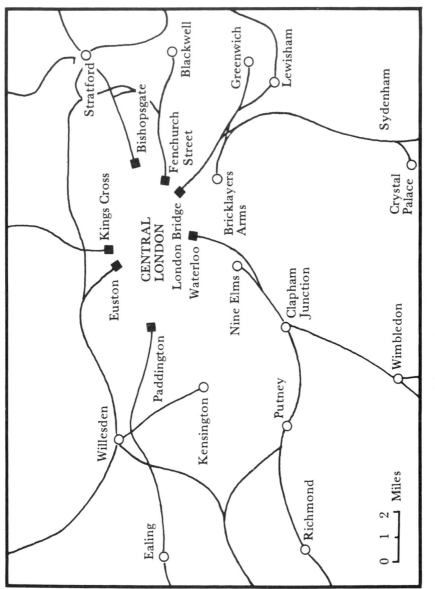

Map of the London area showing railways, 1851

John Scott Russell, *Papa*

But John Scott Russell's fortunes changed quickly. He was appointed Secretary of the Royal Society of Arts. He was a major force in the creation of the Great Exhibition of 1852 in Hyde Park. He became a very competent designer and builder of ships, among which was HMS *Warrior*, the first British ocean-going 'iron-clad', launched in 1860, and he was one of the six businessmen who sponsored the re-building of the Crystal Palace on an open site in Sydenham, not far from his home.

There were four Scott Russell children: Louise, Norman, Rachel, and Alice. They lived in a large house, known as Westwood Lodge, which was surrounded by shrubs, trees and gardens. The Scott Russells kept several servants and entertained a great deal.

John Scott Russell's fortunes turned when he agreed to build the largest ship of the day, the *Great Eastern*, for the powerful industrialist, Isambard Brunel. Problems arose in the construction of the ship, and disagreements with Brunel ended in the liquidation of his business under inspectorship in 1856. Rachel was only eleven.

Her father recovered his financial position slowly. But he suffered great losses again a decade later when he became the middleman in an ill-advised scheme to provide armaments for the State of Massachusetts during the American Civil War. He was subsequently victimized by a kangaroo court conducted by the council of the Institution of Civil Engineers. While Rachel and her sisters were growing up, their father's career seemed to swing on a pendulum from success and wealth to failure and hardship. The fluctuation in Papa's fortunes would have a strong influence upon his daughters' lives. Rachel wrote to Sullivan in 1866:

> *I don't think that in our present 'straitened' circumstances it is right to spend so much money on pleasure. You have no idea how straitened they are or you would quite understand it.*

Nevertheless, John Scott Russell's daughters were all attractive, bright and well-educated. They had all spent some time in schools on the Continent. They loved music and spoke French and German. They possessed, in short, all the qualities that would have made for advantageous marriages. As the years went by, the thought of such marriages became increasingly important to Mrs Scott Russell who had spent enough time worrying about her husband's income to want to see her children well provided for.

> *Mama said to me last night, "It is not the money that makes the happiness . . . but after one has no absolute anxiety about money, one is so much happier on a little . . .".*

Only Alice, Mama's youngest daughter, seemed to be attracted to wealthy young men. Louise was not, and Rachel was certainly not. Rachel was attracted to the young Arthur Sullivan. This clearly worried Mama, for during the 1860s no self-respecting mother would have considered marriage to an unestablished composer to be in any way advantageous.

When he was only eight years old Sullivan had left his parents' home for good. He spent his next four years at a small boarding school in London. When he was twelve he joined the Chapel Royal choir and was 'adopted' by the Reverend Helmore, Master of Her Majesty's Chapel Royal, and his wife with whom he and the other choirboys lived. At sixteen Sullivan went on scholarship to the Mendelssohn Conservatory in Leipzig and there he was taken under the wing of Mrs Barnett, an Englishwoman, whose family was strikingly similar to the Scott Russells.

Mrs John Francis Barnett had moved to the Continent to supervise the musical education of her children. She had two daughters, Rosamund and Clara, and a son, Domenico. They were all students with Sullivan at the Conservatory. Clara remembered Sullivan as "a smiling youth with an oval, olive-tinted face, dark eyes, a large generous mouth, and a thick crop of dark curly hair, which overhung his low forehead".

When he paid his respects to Mamma, which he did promptly, his ingratiating manners appealed to her at once . . . Sullivan's obvious appreciation of the quality of Mamma's hospitality and the gusto with which he attacked the good things on our supper table won Mamma's heart so completely that later he was the only one of our friends who was ever allowed to come on other evenings besides Sunday.

———◆———

It was part of Sullivan's very nature to ingratiate himself with everyone that crossed his path. He always wanted to make an impression, and what is more, he always succeeded in doing it. Whenever some distinguished person came . . .

to visit the Conservatorium, Sullivan always contrived to be on hand to render some little service which brought him to their notice and formed an entering wedge to their acquaintance. In this way he got into personal touch with most of the celebrities ... He was a natural courtier; which did not prevent him, however, from being a very lovable person.

Sullivan was attracted to Rosamund Barnett, the elder sister, but as she was already interested in another young man, Sullivan turned his attention to Clara, who was at first quite taken with him. But as his interest in her was frequently diverted, Clara soon came to realize that Master Sullivan was an incorrigible flirt. When, for example, Madeline Schiller, an attractive and already established concert pianist, entered the Conservatory, Clara recalled:

... it is almost needless to say that [Sullivan] flirted with her as violently as he was wont to do with every newcomer of note. I had long since concluded, however, that these flirtations were only fires of straw which quickly burnt out ...

Fires of straw! How aptly Clara Barnett characterized her young admirer's nature. And what a shame Clara would not be at hand a few years after to warn any subsequent young ladies that the young Sullivan's passions "quickly burnt out".

Sullivan returned from Leipzig in June 1861. In April of the following year, his incidental music to Shakespeare's *The Tempest* was performed at a Crystal Palace concert and its success made him a national celebrity. In the months that followed, Sullivan began to spend more and more time in Sydenham, which had become an important centre for the arts. A number of socially prominent musical families lived there and Sullivan quickly made himself popular with all of them. These families included the Groves, the von Glehns, and of course the Scott Russells. "Sullivan was in and out of these three homes as an ever welcome guest", one of the Glehns recalled, "for he had a charm that was irresistible".

It was George Grove, however, who became Sullivan's most important friend in Sydenham. Grove, who would later edit *Grove's Dictionary of Music & Musicians*, had begun his

George Grove as a young man. He sponsored the performance of Sullivan's early works at the Crystal Palace

career as an engineer. More recently, he had become Secretary of the Crystal Palace Company and Programme Director of the Saturday concerts. In this capacity he had come to know practically every important musician in England and on the Continent. Thus he stood at the head of the inner circle of Sydenham artistic society. Young girls disliked him because he was too prissy. Women distrusted him because his wife was a notorious scandal-monger. But musicians, especially the younger ones, adored him. A young admirer recalled:

The mere thought of him brings a burst of sunshine into the mind. There never was a man of more delightful humour or of a more abounding gaiety and amiability. Friendliness shone from his eyes and from every line of his face. Cheerfulness entered the room with him and stayed even after he had left, so infectious were his spirits.

The highlight of the week in Sydenham, of course, was the concert at the Crystal Palace on Saturday afternoon which George Grove arranged. Thousands of music lovers would flock down by train from London in the morning and return to the city later in the day.

A thousand memories come back of those early concerts at the Crystal Palace of the friends that gathered round "G", in the gallery from which we listened, and the evenings at his house afterwards when he would carry off some of the musicians, and there would be more music in the intimacy of a small circle . . .

Grove would do everything in his power to help a young musician whose talent he thought worthy. He frequently arranged the debuts of young composers and performers at the Crystal Palace. He would then follow the progress of his protegés with great interest. He called them "his children" and indeed, if he could have adopted them, he would have. In 1862, of course, the newest addition to the list of "children" was Arthur Sullivan.

But George Grove was not the only man to befriend Sullivan in those days. Ernest von Glehn later wrote:

[Sullivan] *was for some years an intimate in my old home known as "The Peak" to a wide circle of friends, and he was . . . also a constant visitor at the house of John Scott Russell, the well-known engineer, whose three beautiful and accomplished daughters were on the closest of terms of intimacy with my sisters . . .*

The house on the Peak or Peak Hill Lodge was the home of Ernest von Glehn and his family which included twelve children. Von Glehn had been born in Estonia. He had maintained his Russian contacts and managed a very success-

'The Romans leaving Britain', an oil painting by John Millais, 1866. Alice Scott Russell was the model for the central figure.

ful import business. The Glehns entertained a great deal and were a lively and musical family. One of their daughters, Mimi, went to Germany to study piano with Hans von Bülow. Another of the Glehn children remembered:

At my own home we used to indulge a good deal in private theatricals . . . and on a few occasions Sullivan would act with us — but the memorable occasion was the first (or nearly the first) performance of Cox and Box *at our house, in which Sullivan played Box; Fred Clay, Cox and Norman Scott Russell, Bouncer; while Franklin Taylor officiated as orchestra. Both Sullivan and Clay had voices of great beauty, and this delightful little operetta went with a charm and go which I don't think has been equalled by any other performers since.*

The lyrics to *Cox and Box* were written by Francis Burnand who later became the editor of *Punch*. He was a young Cambridge graduate and a frequent visitor to Sydenham. Frederick Clay was Sullivan's closest friend in London and a composer who would be best remembered for the ballad *I'll Sing Thee Songs of Araby*. Franklin Taylor had been a fellow student of Sullivan's in Leipzig, and would go on to become a popular concert pianist and a distinguished teacher. These were some of the younger people who appeared in Sydenham while Louise, Rachel and Alice Scott Russell were growing up. John Millais, the painter, was another.

The Lehmanns of Westbourne Terrace did not live in Sydenham proper, but they did attend many concerts and parties there. Frederick Lehmann had been born in Hamburg, where he had known Mendelssohn, Liszt and Chopin. He was an excellent violinist. His wife, Nina, who was from an important Scottish literary family, was a brilliant pianist. The Lehmanns were the first socially prominent couple at whose home Sullivan, the natural courtier, was accepted upon his return from Leipzig. It was not long before Sullivan began flirting with Nina Lehmann, who was twelve years his senior.

Thus by the age of twenty-one Sullivan's social life was already rather complex: a flirtatious relationship with Mrs Lehmann, an innocent relationship with the Scott Russell girls, and not such innocent ones with one or two of the women he was meeting in social and Bohemian London.

Ponsonby Castle, sketched from life & from the street by a distinguished Artist —

(The Artist)

A sketch of the house in Ponsonby Street in which Sullivan lived when he first met Rachel in 1863 the artist, Arthur Sullivan. Sullivan sent the rendering to Mrs Lehmann's son on his seventh birthday. (Pierpont Morgan Library)

In 1863 Sullivan was living in an undistinguished lodging in Ponsonby Street. His best friend Frederick Clay, who was the son of a Peer, first introduced Sullivan to 'social' London — that is to say London's bohemian circle and men's clubs.

What was known as bohemian London in the 1860s was in fact a restricted social circle composed primarily of rich people with artistic aspirations and poor people with artistic abilities. Members of the bohemian circle would meet at the theatre, at concerts, at art galleries, and especially at private parties where amateur theatricals and recitals were the order of the day.

The London men's clubs provided a more fraternal way of life for many well-bred and well-connected young men. The clubs were located in large and impressive buildings which were owned by the members. There they could eat, drink, and enjoy the company of other members. If they chose, they could gamble well into the night, every night of the week.

This style of living was beginning to appeal to Sullivan for he loved parties, enjoyed smoking, and was acquiring a taste for gambling. He made a number of friends at the Garrick Club and became quickly popular on the London party circuit, for the young Arthur Sullivan liked nothing better than to sit down at the drawing-room piano and entertain, literally for hours, whenever he had an audience.

Freddie Clay. He was engaged to Alice Scott Russell
while Sullivan was engaged to Rachel

Clay and Sullivan were great friends and it was a delight to get the two of them to the piano and set to improvising à quatre mains — this they could do with something like reciprocal intuition, as if the four hands were worked with one brain.

Sullivan was grateful to Freddie Clay for introducing him to the social whirl of London, and shortly thereafter Clay had cause to be grateful to Sullivan, who introduced him to the Scott Russells in Sydenham. Freddie was received with great warmth at Westwood Lodge, for he was young, charming and a gifted musician. In addition, being the son of a Peer would hardly have passed unnoticed in a family which was having its share of financial troubles. Soon Sullivan and Freddie Clay found themselves journeying to Sydenham every weekend to see Rachel and Alice.

That was in 1864 when Louise, the eldest Scott Russell sister, was spending the autumn at a finishing school in Switzerland. Her absence (conveniently) left only two daughters at home to entertain the two composers. This arrangement worked out well. Rachel and Sullivan were strongly attracted to each other and Freddie Clay and Alice were just as happily matched. Years later, Rachel recalled those days fondly:

I have just been playing The Tempest *through with Lady [Louise]. Oh! darling, it called up such happy times when we sat looking out on the lovely garden bathed in golden sunshine, as happy and blithe as birds and played that love duet while you told me all the passionate words the music was to represent.*

———◆———

. . . all those pleasant times gone — when you used to come down about 4 — and sit chatting with us in the pretty drawing room by the firelight till dinner time — Then the cheery dinner and the music and whist in the evenings!

Sullivan remembered those times with affection too. When he and the girls were not making music, he recalled, they would discuss "painting, poetry, literature and even science until the clock told us that the last train back to London was nearly due" . . . "Those evenings", Sullivan wrote, "were amongst the happiest of my life".

But while these evenings were passing by so happily in Sydenham poor Louise could only read about them in the letters which her sisters wrote to her in Switzerland. And so Louise began her own correspondence with Sullivan from abroad.

> *I suppose I should be exterminated if Mlle. found out that I carry on clandestine correspondence with that article of humanity* [a young man]. *We are such innocent little beings. We talk about our studies, our little quarrels, the weather, the pretty things we have seen. We are none of us out yet because few of us have attained the age of 17 . . .*
>
> *I remain, dear Mr. Sullivan, your — really, I do not know what! — My feelings fight with my propriety.*

Louise was twenty-three years old when that letter was written, and yet it was a childish letter in which she seemed to have entered completely into the world of the seventeen-year-olds at Madamoiselle's. Thus when Louise returned to Sydenham after her year abroad and discovered that during her absence both of her sisters had become romantically involved with the two young composers, she did not seem to mind having been left out. Louise in fact may even have felt more comfortable in watching her sisters' romances than actually having a boyfriend of her own. Louise was the eldest daughter, but for some reason was the least worldly and the most inhibited, and she remained so all her life.

Alice, on the other hand, was the youngest of the three girls, and the most independent and self-confident member of the family. She was a good complement to Freddie Clay, who was easy-going, well-to-do, and hardly consumed with ambition.

Arthur Sullivan was the opposite of Freddie Clay, that is to say, he was poor and determined to succeed; and in the latter quality he was a good match for Rachel who was the middle daughter and the most competitive member of her family. Rachel wanted Sullivan to realize his full potential

Twilight, a romance for piano which Sullivan dedicated to Rachel at her request – or perhaps demand
(Pierpont Morgan Library)

without delay. She was determined to share the glory with him and she had little hesitation in admitting it!

Oh, strain every nerve for my sake — women love to be proud of their friends — and I don't think you know how ambitious I am. I want you to write something for which all the world must acknowledge your talent . . .

There is no time like the present — and you are in the frame of mind to do something great if you are ever to do it — Remember, I have staked my all on you — win or fail? First or nothing I answer . . .

Rachel was an excellent pianist, and had she lived in another century she would no doubt have been a professional musician herself. But she was living in an age in which few women embarked on careers, and it must have been a source of constant frustration for her to know that her role in life would most likely see her confined to the home.

It is always better for men because they must work even if their hearts be breaking, and we must make work for ourselves which nothing but a vague sense of duty renders necessary.

Rachel understood that the only way in which she could realize her potential would be to marry a musician and guide and influence his work. Sullivan, she decided, was the musician she must marry. ". . . in every note you write" she told him, "my soul is with yours".

Do come my own one on Friday night and bring your work and you can write after we are all in bed, and all Saturday and I will sit and coo by you and cover you with my passionate love kisses. Besides, I want to coo some of birdie's self into the overture — Oh! you must write me into it . . .

Sullivan, however, had a curiously lazy streak about him when it came to composing and Rachel was determined to rid him of it.

I have said so often you could and will be the first musician of the time . . . You have the tools all ready — you have

18

*the prize before you — will you mould a beautiful form
with all your soul and your strength — The best — a thing
before which all shall fall down — no rather to which all
shall look up — and which shall raise them all and win for
yourself a name and a place among the great men who
have gone before.*

Rachel was driving Sullivan as hard as she possibly could
and, curiously, Sullivan was finding this kind of encouragement strangely stimulating.

*Does my voice thrill through you dear? I wish I had you
here that I could talk to you. There is nothing you cannot
do if you will only will it — No man ever had such a
chance as you, never — you have a name already and
scarcely any rivals.*

Under Rachel's spell Sullivan took a new look at a series of
sketches for a symphony which he had made in Ireland two
summers before. With fresh inspiration from Rachel he
finished it quickly, and in March 1866, was able to secure its
performance at the Crystal Palace. The work was a great
success at its première, and the critic of the *Musical Times*
called it "the best musical work . . . for a long time produced
by any English composer". Rachel was ecstatic. Through
Sullivan she was beginning to realize her own musical ambi-
tions and there was little doubt in her mind that in the slow
movement Sullivan was speaking directly to *her.*

*Arthur, my darling, you know that I glory in pure music,
and you cannot know the exultant feeling there is in
birdie's heart when she hears those glorious harmonies
and knows that it is her darling's beautiful love speaking
to all who hear . . .*

————◆————

*We had . . . the C Minor Symph: Beethoven which they
played divinely — one thing which I longed for — someone's hand to hold — and a pair of dark eyes to turn mine
on when the pleasure was too great.*

Music, love and Arthur Sullivan were all becoming one in
Rachel's mind.

The Musical World.

"The worth of Art appears most eminent in Music, since it requires no material, no subject-matter, whose effect must be deducted: it is wholly form and power, and it raises and ennobles whatever it expresses."—*Göthe.*

SUBSCRIPTION, FREE BY POST, 20s. PER ANNUM

Payable in advance by Cash or Post-Office Order to DUNCAN DAVISON & CO., 244, Regent Street, London, W.

[*Registered for Transmission Abroad.*]

VOL. 44—No. 10. SATURDAY, MARCH 10, 1866. Price { 4d. Unstamped. 5d. Stamped.

Advertisement in *Musical World* for the first performance of Sullivan's symphony at the Crystal Palace on 10 March 1866

In 1866 and 1867, the years of Rachel's greatest influence, Sullivan wrote two overtures, one symphony and a concerto. This was more than ninety per cent of the purely symphonic music he composed during his entire life. But even these works were not flowing easily from his pen. A few months after the première of his symphony, Sullivan wanted to abandon a commission he had received from the Norwich Festival for want of symphonic inspiration. Rachel wrote:

> ... my pet, _please_ write the overture and don't keep saying you _would write songs if you had the words_ — Do the overture for me as a pis aller _instead of vainly longing for words._

By the age of twenty-four Sullivan had already begun to succumb to what was to be his life-long dependence on _words_ as his source of musical inspiration, and Rachel was quick to realize where his real strength lay.

> I want you to write an opera — such an opera — and I feel it must be done this winter — a grand and vigorous great work.

The first part of Tennyson's poem _Idylls of the King_ had recently been published — the tales of Enid, Lynette, Vivien and Guinevere. Rachel was fascinated by these romances in which women played a far more central role in life (than they did in Sydenham). She decided that Sullivan's opera should be entitled _Guinevere._

To Rachel, Guinevere represented the height of romantic love. Love so strong that it could sweep away all barriers, even those of right and wrong. Love so deep that the lovers would lie, deceive and betray for it, and of course be punished. Throughout her relationship with Sullivan, Rachel seems to have maintained a curious identification with Guinevere.

> Darling, I am so interested in Guinevere — I feel as though it were the thing and oh, birdie I care dreadfully that it should be a splendid work and a success . . .
>
> The only thing I fear for are Guinevere's and Launcelot's love songs. They must not be too pure — or they won't be in keeping with their characters.

Rachel needn't have worried about *that*. Sullivan's bohemian life in London was not filled with an excess of purity. He was far from discreet and his behaviour had long since begun to cause comment. Frequently he would party well into the night, then take a late train down to Sydenham and, finding everyone asleep in Westwood Lodge, he would go away angry.

I cannot think how you can go on living the life you do — going to miserable sickly London parties, smoking half the night through — and then getting up seedy and limp and unfit for any good honest work.

———◆———

Don't sit up till one or two in the morning smoking — it is <u>*ruin*</u> *to your health and to your work . . . one of the things people say now, and with justice against <u>it</u> is that you will be an old broken down man at forty . . .*

Rachel's letters were filled with this kind of moralizing. (She had apparently heard a good deal of it from her mother.) It was hardly likely to have any effect on Sullivan, for he had learned he could still continue to live his 'other' life in London *while courting Rachel*. He would pretend to be a lost soul floundering in the wicked city, with only the words of his beloved to protect him.

You must be strong enough to deny yourself for me and give up that miserable sitting up late at night and all the rest of it which is simply <u>ruin</u> morally and physically . . .

Rachel might, of course, have forgiven some of Sullivan's behaviour on the grounds of immaturity. But she could never forgive his flirtations with other women.

. . . and how fortunate it is that I trust you quite implicitly, otherwise, I should be inclined to think you have deceived me, for you were seen in Bond Street on Saturday in a hansom with Lady Katherine.

I try to think it was an accident because I cannot believe you would not have told me. Anyway I don't like it . . .

———◆———

I don't trust you enough, birdie, to let you go to see Mrs. Lehmann — so you must give that up, my own sweet one. You know you told me you could not trust yourself when you get naughty — and darling, I never could love you again if I thought any other woman had any power over you.

It was hardly surprising that Rachel was becoming jealous. By the middle of 1866 Sullivan's life-style was beginning to pose a problem which may well have precipitated a crisis had it not been for two unexpected events which brought Rachel and Sullivan suddenly closer together. Rachel's father found himself in severe financial trouble, and Sullivan's father died without warning.

Tom Sullivan, centre, the composer's father; note similarity in appearance to George Grove

Old Thomas Sullivan had been a kind and loving father. He had been bandmaster at the Royal Military Academy, Sandhurst, and his son's first musical instructor. He had taught young Arthur to play six band instruments before he was eight years old.

Thomas Sullivan never made very much money, but whatever he failed to give his children materially, he had made up for in warmth. He continually made sacrifices for his family and took a second job to pay for his son's continued schooling in Leipzig. It had always been Arthur Sullivan's strongest desire to be successful so that his father might see some return for his sacrifices, and spend the end of his days in comfort. Now that goal would never be realized and the young composer was desolate. He wrote to Mrs. Lehmann:

> *My dear, dear Father, whom I loved so passionately and who returned my love a hundredfold if that were possible! Oh, it is so hard — it is so terribly hard to think that I shall never see his dear face again, or hear his cheery voice saying, 'God bless you, my boy!' . . .*
>
> *I am able to be strong all day for my poor Mother's sake, who is nearly broken hearted . . . but at night, when I am alone, then the wound bursts out, and I think of him and his tender love and care for me, and his pride in all I did — and now he is gone for ever, and how do I know where or whether we shall meet again?*
>
> *Perhaps he can look upon me and see all I do; and please God I will try and never do anything that will make him turn away his head and regret that he left me alone here . . .*

For the first time in his life Arthur Sullivan was experiencing emotions which were frightening and foreign to his previously buoyant nature.

> *In great pain of this kind one holds out one's hands in an agony to see if anyone will clutch them and press them even for a moment only, and it would be sad to hold them out in vain.*

Rachel, who was nearby, was willing to provide the necessary warmth and understanding.

> *... my darling, you have more need of tenderness than I have, and please God I will be good and strong and always be ready to comfort you when you need it.*

At the same time Rachel's home also was in a state of upheaval. John Scott Russell, since his rift with the Institution of Civil Engineers the year before, had been having difficulty in finding work in England. Rachel wrote:

> *... darling, we are all <u>low</u>. Our affairs are very blue and life, bare life, is a hard struggle just now, and we are all depressed by it. Of course I need not ask you not to breathe this to <u>anyone</u> else.*

Things in fact had become so bad that Papa and Mama had begun to speak of moving abroad permanently. Rachel was terrified. She could not bear the thought of being separated from Sullivan and she knew that if her parents moved to the Continent she would not be permitted to remain behind in England — unless of course she were married.

Rachel and Sullivan had spoken of marriage many times, but only in terms of the future. There were a number of obstacles to their immediate marriage, and one of them of course was money. "I think if you had any *settled* thing like a conductorship", Rachel wrote, "there would be no opposition." But Sullivan had no 'settled thing' in 1867. He had an income of approximately £100 a year as Music Director of St. Michael's, a church in Chester Square, to which were added whatever royalties he received from the sale of his songs. He had his Mother to support, and he was living well beyond his means as it was. Rachel knew that if she were to announce her engagement to him now, her parents would certainly object.

The financial pressures on the Scott Russells were severe, and sometime in May of 1867 their plans to move abroad began to crystallize. There was talk of putting Westwood Lodge up for auction and a short family visit to Paris was hastily arranged.

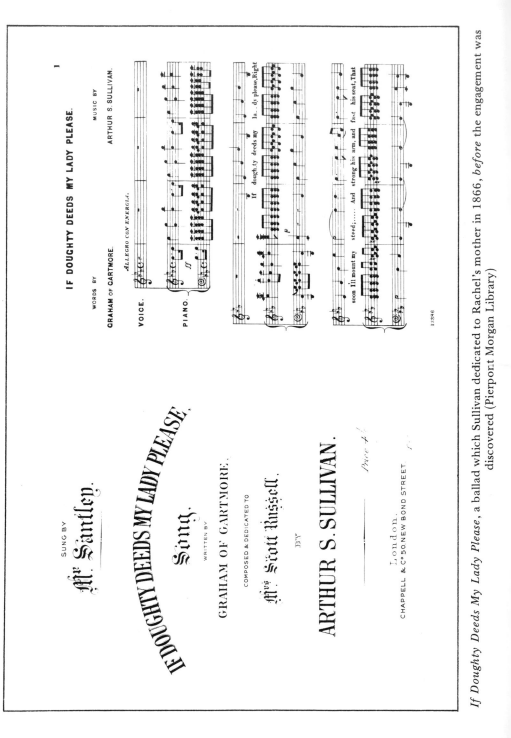

If Doughty Deeds My Lady Please, a ballad which Sullivan dedicated to Rachel's mother in 1866, *before* the engagement was discovered (Pierpont Morgan Library)

About a week before the Paris trip (probably on Friday, 3rd May) Rachel went up to London. She and Sullivan spent the evening together, and late at night, Sullivan took her back to Sydenham on the train when most probably they talked about the future. Rachel would have been very frightened, and Sullivan understanding. Their lives were already completely intertwined. They undoubtedly spoke of marriage. For now that Rachel's family was planning to move abroad, she needed Sullivan more than ever. But could he love her and her alone after all of his 'flirtations'? "Do you remember that train ride?" Rachel wrote later, "you literally conquered and subdued me there." There is no way of knowing what Sullivan might have said to win Rachel that night, but one remark survives. "And I asked myself", Rachel wrote quoting Sullivan, "is your heart great enough for a love which never tires? And the answer came full and strong without a doubt, Yes, strong enough to last forever is my love!" Sullivan probably said many similar things to Rachel that evening and Rachel apparently believed him.

When the train arrived in Sydenham, Sullivan led her to a spot that he knew well, and there Rachel, convinced that Arthur Sullivan really loved her, and convinced that he would one day marry her, desperately in need of his affection, in spite of the havoc to be wreaked if Mama should ever find out, at last allowed him to make love to her.

And after that only two things changed: Rachel became a traitor to her family, and Arthur Sullivan began to save her letters.

Come to me my darling, I hold out my arms to you. Oh! come to them and let me forget the world and all its griefs in your great love.

CHAPTER TWO

Mama Takes Over

(May 1867 — December 1867)

I would see by what Freddie said that he thinks I have no physical passion in me — and please don't ever undeceive him — it is a thing you created and called out and between you and me let it rest a secret.
— Rachel to Sullivan

Sullivan in 1864, shortly after he met Rachel

Oh! my own sweet love — if I could sit alone with you for days and weeks and do nothing else but pour out my love upon you, all the time, I would not show you how tenderly and passionately I love you. My own one love, when shall I see you and get a kiss from your dear lips and see the love that I live for welling up out of the depths of your eyes?

Rachel had finally given herself to Sullivan, and from that moment on she thought about him continually. She wrote to him once or twice a day. She began to sign her letters Passion Flower, a very apt self-description, and she became very quickly hurt whenever Sullivan could not see her.

Unfortunately, however, it was May, and Sullivan had many commitments for the summer. He had been commissioned by the Philharmonic Society to compose an overture for their concert on 3rd June. He had already sketched out some themes for a work based on Walter Scott's *Marmion*, but he had barely begun to score them when he took on a new assignment. Frank Burnand talked him into conducting a charity matinée of *Cox and Box* at the Adelphi Theatre, which meant that Sullivan would have to orchestrate the operetta immediately. As the piece had never been performed publicly the accompaniment had never been written down. The performance at the Adelphi was scheduled for Saturday, 11th May, leaving Sullivan only five days to score nine songs, some of which were very long and complicated.

Rachel, however, was leaving for Paris in a few days. It would be the first major separation since the beginning of their relationship. Sullivan of course was far more interested in spending time with her than in composing. Rachel was going to be gone for *one whole week*! She begged Sullivan to take at least a day off and visit her in Paris. He said that he would try to, but when Rachel left he still had most of *Cox and Box* to score, as well as *Marmion*.

Rachel left for Paris towards the end of the week. That Friday Sullivan stayed up all night. He barely finished *Cox and Box* in time for a band rehearsal on Saturday morning. He then conducted the matinée and returned to his rooms in a state of total exhaustion.

My darling heart.
                    Would it be possible
for me to have "my box" on Tuesday
for "Faust" with Lucca & Mario?
            A letter by every post! &
such scraps. But I feel I
cannot write. I can only lay
my brown tired head on the —
of resting place it knows & I
feel your love & your hot kisses
on my face. Darling Darling. Come.
                    your own little
                    Passion Flower.

Letter from Rachel to Sullivan signed 'Passion Flower'
(Pierpont Morgan Library)

On Sunday Sullivan ought to have resumed work on *Marmion*, but he decided instead to ride down to Westbourne Terrace and spend the day with Mrs Lehmann. He would get a fresh start on *Marmion* the following morning.

From Monday on, however, Sullivan was continuously busy. *Marmion* had to be completed in time for the rehearsals about 27th May. It was already 13th May. He barely had time to scrawl a line to Rachel in Paris explaining that he could not possibly take a day off to visit her. Rachel was annoyed. She felt that the very least she merited during this first separation from her lover was one day of attention and a £3 return ticket. But when she got back to Sydenham she became even more annoyed. There was a Philharmonic concert that week and Sullivan was not even planning to take her. *Marmion* was ruining her social life. *Then* she discovered that *Marmion* notwithstanding, Sullivan had managed to visit Mrs Lehmann the Sunday before, and that was too much!

Mrs Nina Lehmann and her husband Frederick (British Library). Sullivan's flirtation with her almost destroyed his relationship with Rachel

Bournes " don't recollect acting"
your found for a
some time afterwards "
Loves fame

Several Days afterwards "

No 2.

Song. Bourness.

Allegretto Pastorale.

Flauti

Oboe

Clarinetti in C.

Fagotto

Corni

A page from the score of *Cox and Box* in Sullivan's hand

Dear little bird,

I am so dreadfully hurt at your not coming down to see me that I can hardly write to you. I cried myself to sleep last night and today I feel very sad.

I really think that instead of coming down here so <u>*absurdly*</u> *often as you have been doing, you might have worked so as to have had a little free time for me — but I observe that when pleasure or work come across you, I always go to the wall. So that though you could find plenty of time to come here and chat and – – – – over the fire, you could only find time to scrawl me a few lines to Paris.*

We shall only be here about a month longer and when we live abroad you will have plenty of time to follow your own sweet will in London.

By the by, you better rush down at once to see Mrs Lehmann so as to have some one to console you when we are gone.

When you are <u>*quite*</u> *at leisure, I want to have a long earnest talk with you about things which will concern your future and mine, and till I have settled those things I cannot settle down.*

Perhaps you could come down here on Sunday, as I daresay you can arrange to do for me what you did for your own pleasure last Sunday.

I am not at all well and I shall go to see Dr Kidd on Saturday — that sea voyage nearly killed me.

I am so sore and unhappy that I cannot write any more. This overture of yours is the only piece you ever wrote that I don't care a straw about. They may hiss it for all I care . . .

When Sullivan received this letter he became just as angry as Rachel. She knew how busy he was. How could she possibly have expected a visit from him in Paris? Sullivan read her letter over again. He was not amused. *This overture of yours is the only piece you ever wrote that I don't care a straw about.* If that was how Rachel felt about his music, Sullivan thought, she certainly didn't have to listen to it, and he sent her a furious reply (now lost). When Rachel received it she became predictably hysterical.

In bed

Friday

*My own own love — my precious darling — oh my darling!
I have been punished for that wicked wicked letter I wrote
you — punished so bitterly — be kind as you are powerful
and do not punish me any more.   Darling I come to you
and lay my head down on your knees and beg of you to
kiss my poor little face and forgive me — Do darling . . .*

*. . . Darling, I have cried my eyes out for the longing I
have to see and feel you — Oh my darling, my life's love,
come to me, <u>do</u> <u>do</u> come to me only just to kiss me and let
me hear the voice that I love saying the words that give me
new life.*

*Ah, my darling you cannot be angry with me — because
I <u>love</u> you — and love, love like ours forgives <u>all</u> things or
it is not love. You should know me too well to be angry at
my anger — You should know "Poor little bird, her heart
must be very sore to let her hurt mine like this." — That is
just what it is my own one.*

*Darling I am ill again and we don't know what is the
matter. I am sick and weary and I feel as if my heart would
break if you did not come to me. It is so hard to crave for
you in this heart-sinking way and feel that you will not
come . . .*

*Ah birdie, life is so short and we must not let there be
any bitterness between us — Do forgive me. It is worse for
me to have written such a letter and turned your love into
anger than it was for you to receive it.*

*Oh darling when will you take me to you <u>forever</u> —
I will never go away from you again — I cannot bear it —
and I want you to take me to my "home" — or rather to
<u>your</u> home and make it mine.*

*Perhaps now you will not have me. Am I too naughty
to take home — Could you not live with me?*

*Try me darling and make me as sweet as you are
yourself.*

*Oh! darling, darling, come to me and bring your work
and you will <u>see</u> if I love it or no.*

Come to me — because I love you. Come to me because
you love me. Come to me because I am ill and weary and
only rest in your arms and kisses from your dear mouth
will make me well.

My heart's dream you little know the force of passionate
fierce love I have for you — and yet I will be as tender as
your little bird should be. Oh Arthur, forgive me and you
shall do what you like with me. I will go to you, will be
your wife. Anything, anything, only to be with you and
hear that you are mine as I am yours.

Your passionately loving little
Bird.

Sullivan did not reply to this letter.

Over the weekend he finished *Marmion* and had the
orchestral parts copied out in time for the first rehearsal.
When completed, *Marmion* proved to be a picturesque and
faintly Scottish, spirited and well orchestrated piece of work
and W. G. Cusins, the Philharmonc conductor, was pleased
with it.

With the pressure of work now off him Sullivan could
begin to relax. He wrote to Rachel, beginning "My dearest
wife". Then he scratched out the words and started again.
It didn't much matter what he wrote after that. Rachel knew
that she had been forgiven, and that Sullivan was thinking
of the future and not of the past. They had survived their
first crisis.

Crisis number two, however, was near at hand. Rachel
had a tendency to push Sullivan too far, and in one of her
letters, she gives an excellent example of the tone in which
Mrs Scott Russell, or for that matter, any Victorian mother,
might have spoken to her daughters.

Now fold your hands penitently and listen: You have
written a New Anthem and two Hymns — and not only
have I not got them, but I never even heard of them till
the Glehns told me. Now darling I ask you, is this right?
No, you say, it is not — and do you look sorry? Yes, very.
Well then, I will kiss and make friends, but it must not
occur again.

Mama may have found this approach effective in the rearing

of four small children, but Arthur was hardly likely to respond to it. He continued to see other women in London, and this disturbed Rachel tremendously.

It ought to be impossible for us, even in thought, to be unfaithful for one minute and darling, till our love is perfect like that I cannot marry you, for it would not last.

What troubled Rachel the most of course was Sullivan's flirtation with Mrs Lehmann, who was a close friend of her family's. At the beginning of June a party was to be held at the Lehmann's.

I would not go down to the Lehmanns on Saturday if I thought there were the least shadow of a danger for me! But you see, women of any sort or breed have such a physical influence over you that you cannot conceive how utterly and hopelessly cold I am since I love you.

Sullivan of course felt perfectly justified in seeing Mrs Lehmann whenever he chose to, and he made this perfectly clear to Rachel in another strongly-worded letter (also lost). She replied:

Of course your letter was written to give me pain and it will be a satisfaction to know how perfectly well it succeeded. I suppose the great object of love is to teach one to bear heartache without wincing and I think in time I shall learn. I have just read over one of your old good noble letters to reassure myself and to be quite sure that what I am loving so passionately is worth loving. — I have no doubt you spent a delightful <u>night</u> with Mrs. Lehmann and I only hope the recollection of the <u>road near the river</u> only a few short days ago did not haunt you.

I don't think I care very much. Go and pet Kathy and then go down and do likewise to Mrs. L. or anyone else. It is only one disillusionment more. It will never change me. You might be as wicked as you liked and break all the vows and protestations you have made holding me in your arms and looking straight into my eyes — and it would not make me think I had a right to do likewise. — I still believe you will not be able to kiss me and call me your dearest love and look quite straight at me out of your dear eyes if you have betrayed my love.

39

Sullivan's affair with Rachel was still in its first month and he had already had several arguments with her. "You see, she is so very peculiar", Louise wrote to Sullivan some time later. "I do not think that she *can* love evenly. Passionate outbursts and then coolings down — that will always be her way. But then I think that suits you." Rachel's recent letter apparently came under the heading of a passionate outburst.

George Grove's house in lower Sydenham. Westwood Lodge was probably somewhat similar though larger

In the beginning of July one more problem arose. Sullivan was going to Paris as Music Director of the British delegation to the Paris Exhibition. He would be gone for two weeks. His departure made Rachel somewhat anxious for she still could not bear to be without him for more than a few days at a time. As he was to be gone for two whole weeks Rachel insisted that he write to her regularly.

Sullivan left. Rachel waited expectantly, but there were no letters for her. Days passed. Rachel was disturbed. Why was Sullivan not writing? A week went by — still no word from Paris. Rachel was very upset, and by the middle of the second week, her anxiety had become readily apparent to her mother, and Mama asked her what was wrong.

Under the circumstances, of course, the last thing that Rachel wanted was to tell her mother what was upsetting her. But Mama had been monitoring Rachel's changes of humour for several weeks, and she finally demanded (and got) a full explanation.

No letter, unfortunately, survives to explain exactly how Mrs Scott Russell persuaded Rachel to tell her about her relationship with Sullivan. But when Mama finally learned the truth, she was predictably horrified. Sullivan had been her most trusted visitor. Now he was planning to marry her daughter! Sullivan the penniless composer! Sullivan the bandmaster's son! "I trusted you like none other but God!" Mama cried, "and you have deceived me!" Later Rachel described the scene:

> *I spoke to Mama tonight, or rather she spoke to me. You have no idea and I had none till tonight, of the force of the passion there is in her. I cannot tell you all that passed, but her decisive words were, "I will die sooner than let you marry him and mind, it will break your father's heart and mine — he would never recover [from] it."*
>
> *. . . I see now that it would always have been the same and that if we had told her when you first told me, the only effect would have been to have forbidden you the house . . .*

"I will never marry him without your consent", Rachel told her mother that evening, "but I will *never* marry anyone else."

Then, in complete defiance of her mother's attitude, she wrote to him: "Darling, it may have been *wrong*. — but it has given us two years of rare happiness which *I* at least shall never forget nor regret."

The next day Mrs Scott Russell wrote to Sullivan herself.

> *My dear Mr. Sullivan,*
> *It has come upon me with a shock to learn that you could not be content to remain on merely the terms of intimate friendship in this family which have so long*

subsisted with us, I believed, to much enjoyment and advantage to all parties.

It grieves me to tell you that under <u>no</u> circumstances could I ever consent to a different relation and therefore I ask you — if you <u>cannot</u> bring yourself to be satisfied with that which has hitherto subsisted, to abstain from coming here till you can do so — and to cease all correspondence.

I grieve that I reposed in you a confidence to which you were not equal . . .

A day later Sullivan replied in similar terms:

You must have known me long and intimately enough to be aware that in some matters I am as earnest and dedicated as yourself . . . Therefore, although it is with indescribable grief and pain that I do so, I must, of necessity . . . stay away from the house altogether. But do not by this be deceived into thinking for one instant that my feelings are changed or that in any sort of way I forego my determination to marry your daughter. So long as she holds to the engagement and is of the same inclination, so long shall I feel myself both bound by love and honour to look upon her as my future wife . . .

When Mama read this letter she went directly in to Rachel and announced that her daughter was never to see or write to Arthur Sullivan again. When Rachel heard this, she promptly wrote to him.

Sunday

My own darling, my own one love —

"I put my hands in yours and looking straight into your dear dear eyes, I say <u>True</u> <u>unto</u> <u>death</u> Arthur." Those words are said now again with all my soul now, that a cloud has come over our Sun and the course of our true love is not running smooth . . .

Do not fear darling — if ever I doubted my love for you — if ever I felt that you were <u>necessary</u> to my happiness and my life — it is now that I <u>know</u> that you <u>are</u> my <u>dearest</u>

42

My dear Mr. Sullivan

It has come upon me
with a shock to learn that
you should not be content
to remain on merely the terms
of intimate friendship in
this family which have so
long subsisted with (as I believe)
so much enjoyment & advantage
to all parties

It grieves me to tell
you that under *no*
circumstances could I
ever consent to a different
relation and therefore I
ask you — if you cannot

'It has come upon me with something of a shock . . .'. Mrs Scott Russell's letter to Sullivan upon learning of her daughter's engagement to him. (Pierpont Morgan Library)

bring yourself to be satisfied
with that which has hitherto
subsisted to abstain from
coming here till you can do
so and to cease all correspondence. —

I grieve that I reposed
in you a confidence to which
you were not equal. I did it
in absolute good faith
partly believing that you
quite understood it — partly
believing that you had
other views for yourself —
& partly relying with entire
trust on the assurances
given me from time to
time that my confidence
was not being abused. —

You cannot have more
pain in reading this than
I have in writing it for it
is with a great effort that
I grieve any one — but yet
do not believe that I could
ever relent for I cannot
conceive of any circumstance
that would make me for
one moment waver in this
fixed resolve —

believe me Revd Mr Sullivan
to remain
Your faithful friend
Henriette Scott Russell

Westwood Lodge
29th July —

as and anxid plays

as obligation to me if I asked, for I know history aims
I must justify the knowledge of in acting from a love which he has
a deand home true & where now all the happiness of a life lies.

You offer me two alternatives; either to remain on terms of
friendly with your daughter, or to carry all communication with her.
Now you must have known me long fortunately enough
to be aware that no in some matter I am so correct to

Draft of Sullivan's reply to Mrs Scott Russell's letter barring him from her house. (Pierpont Morgan Library)

and my best, and that my life is dark and sad and lifeless without you. Therefore my darling, if your love is all you thought it, and if you can stand this trial and bear such hard waiting as this will be, just put your arms around me and say "my own one, my darling love, till death us do part."

I will write to you constantly darling. I have promised not to marry you until they consent, but that is all. Love you I will better than all the world — and love letters you shall have by hundreds to keep your courage up. I am estranged from my mother for I can never forget the cold hard things she said that night. Have courage darling. Still work for me. I am waiting for you always there true as steel and in time if we leave it quite, I am sure they will get reconciled to it — especially now they know I am in earnest . . .

Don't tell anyone of this — it is only a storm and will pass away. Keep up your courage my own one — and write to me daily a long long letter that I may have it to help me tomorrow. Oh! my love, tell me all I want to hear — that this lonely aching may go out of my heart — and tell me if you can be faithful to me for ever.

Oh, Arthur, I put my arms round you and kiss you darling as I never kissed you before. God bless and keep you my own one — and some day Arthur I will stand before you waiting till you hold out your arms and clasp me in them for ever.

> *Your own one I am*
> *true until death*

Rachel charged Sullivan with a special responsibility.

Remember: I leave my honour in your hands. You must burn all my letters as soon as you read them.

Rachel had no intention of giving Sullivan up merely because her mother wanted her to. He may have been banned from the house, but she had not been confined to it. As long as her freedom of movement had not been limited by the discovery of her intrigue, she was determined to continue it in any way she could. Her relationship with Sullivan was about to enter a dramatic new phase. She would carry on her romance surreptitiously. She would see him in private. She would have a secret lover — as Guinevere had.

Mama of course was quite unaware of Rachel's plans, and attempted to take advantage of Sullivan's absence to promote another young man whom she fleetingly hoped might capture her daughter's affections. His name was Harry Wynne. [He may have been related to a Welsh soprano named Edith Wynne, who appeared occasionally on concert programmes with Sullivan.]

Harry Wynne, unfortunately, was making his entrance into the Scott Russell household at a very inopportune time. Rachel had explained her plans to go on seeing Sullivan in secret to her closest friends and they had begun rallying to her aid. Everyone wanted to help! Freddie Clay (who was still permitted to visit Alice) started bringing Rachel's letters from Sullivan in London, while Louise took Rachel's letters *to* Sullivan out of the house to the post-box! But there was one other friend of the family who was promising to be more helpful than anyone in promoting the clandestine romance.

I have had a long talk with Mr. Grove who came here to see how the fat was getting on in the fire! He says I look very well and jolly ... though I want dreadfully to see you.

George Grove of course had known the young lovers for a long time. He was aware of the blind adoration that Rachel felt for her young composer, and he was acquainted too with the 'other life' that Sullivan was leading in London. Grove had also observed a few of the stormier episodes in Rachel's relationship with Sullivan and, now that a crisis had arisen, he apparently told Rachel all that there was to know about Sullivan's character.

I get such pangs about you — as for instance when Mr. Grove said you told him such things about yourself and that he did not think you knew what "devotion" meant — Oh! then I thought — Is it possible that there are things which I do not know of and which he hides from me?

The answer was a resounding yes, and Rachel knew it.

49

Sullivan had already told her that he met with temptation every day in London. Even her sister Louise knew about Sullivan's 'temptations'. She later wrote:

> *Oh Darling, don't touch pitch, don't even look at it. Put away from you what is unlovely, and do not desecrate the sacred and beautiful expression of love.*

Who the other women in Sullivan's life were, and how often he saw them, is not known. But Rachel's letters contain an endless number of requests that Sullivan be true to *her*:

> *Oh! love me, Arthur — and do be <u>true</u> to me — true and faithful darling even in little things.*

———◆———

> *Be true and pure my darling, faithful my heart, and birdie will come to you . . .*

———◆———

> *Good night, darling. May God put some of His infinite love and <u>purity</u> into your heart and make it steadfast and true.*

Now that George Grove had repeated to Rachel his warning about Sullivan's lifestyle, there was nothing more he could do but let events take their natural course. Rachel lost no time in indicating to Sullivan just what the natural course was to be:

> *. . . when you write, let it always be either at night or through Mr. <u>Grove</u>. I <u>must</u> hear from you — hear all you do and think and feel — if my darling loves me and if he is <u>true</u> and <u>good</u> and <u>noble</u>. Write <u>everything</u> to me as you would talk — long diaries — and send them through Mr. Grove to me.*

And so it was that Rachel's romance finally became completely dependent upon what would be its most enduring aspect, the correspondence. Previously the letters had played a relatively minor role in the relationship; now they would dominate it. The Victorian Era was the age of great correspondences. The post was very quick and dependable. Rachel knew when the mail deliveries arrived, and she would often go down to the post office and wait for them. A kind letter from Sullivan would make her day. A cruel one would destroy it. Sullivan's letters to Rachel were becoming as important as Sullivan had been himself. And Rachel expected *her* letters to Sullivan to have just as much meaning to him.

Do you still rejoice when you see my letters, coo over them and talk to your little bird? Do you my love, my love . . .

———◆———

I know you will kiss this letter before you put it by, because I feel it to be exactly like myself — and of course you would kiss me if you had a chance.

———◆———

I remember quite well your telling me what a thrill it gave you seeing the well known letters lying on the table waiting for you.

This new relationship by post, however, was not in the best interests of the romance. Rachel had already begun to deny several truths about Sullivan. Since meetings were forbidden she began to see him — in her letters — exactly as she wanted to see him; as if she were communicating with a fantasy Sullivan that she had created in her mind — a Sullivan who loved her exclusively and was devoted to her slightest whim. Many of the letters written that summer suggest this. The *old* Sullivan, the Sullivan who had so often ignored her or made her jealous, had been barred from her house and, for the most part, from her thoughts as well. Whenever Rachel felt lonely now, she would pour out her heart to her *ideal* Sullivan in a letter and he (she fantasized) would understand.

Oh! My heart's darling, my own love — To be in your arms — to lay my head close to yours — to feel your kisses on my face! Has it all been a dream? Is it possible it was ever there? And oh! My God, will it ever be true again?

She would also direct her ideal to pour out his heart to her:

A little while ago I told you my courage might fail and

*that I might write and ask for all the old burning passion-
ate unfailing love — and you wrote and said that I should
in return get a letter which should warm me forever more.
Will it come?*

But the pastime of correspondence was hardly limited to
Rachel. In a very short time her sisters were drawn into it,
and all three of the Scott Russell girls became avid letter
writers. After a while they began to write to each other's
friends and the letters which they received were practically
public property.

Several evenings a week the three sisters would sit around
the study table reading, writing and sharing their letters.
Rachel even enjoyed the letters that Sullivan was writing to
Louise (or "Lady" as she was called within the family).

*Don't leave off writing to Lady, darling; she is very fond
of your letters, and perhaps — do you think — if you did
not "faire amour" to me quite so much in them?*

Occasionally, however, Sullivan would turn to Louise for
sympathy and nothing would annoy Rachel more.

*Write as you choose to Lady. Pour out the depths of your
heart to her — Show her all my letters to you . . . explain
to her minutely all the wants in my character — I will
never ask to see any of your letters to her.*

For the most part, however, Louise and Rachel got along
well together, and enjoyed sharing each other's correspondence. Louise, who still had no romantic interest of her own,
was perfectly happy to be a vicarious participant in Rachel's
romance. For in addition to exchanging letters with Sullivan,
she often accompanied the lovers as a 'chaperone'. It probably
amused Sullivan to have a romance with one sister while
flirting with another, for he could, when he chose to, play all
three sisters off against each other with consummate skill.

*Lady and I are both a "little hurt" because you called
Dickie [Alice] "such a dear" — now you know we cannot
care for your expressions of affection if you lavish them
on everyone — and that is an expression which is my
property — and she is certainly not a dear . . .*

New Years Day

My dear Arthur. Thank you many many times for yr dear loving letter. I thought I shld hear from you & it gave me deep pleasure to read yr kind words. I still feel amazed, but very truly happy & content. I feel perfectly sure of him & as if no sorrow could

One of two surviving letters to Sullivan from Alice Scott Russell. She signed herself 'Little Maiden'. (Pierpont Morgan Library)

touch me beside him —
We may meet it seems &
I am truly glad as it
can only do us good, &
soon it may be more
difficult — I am nearer now
to you, & If God wills it
we shall all four be
happy together. My happiness
could never be quite complete
if you & Chennie were not

-gether. But you are both brave & I trust it may all end well & soon too. God bless you Arthur & make this a Happy bright good New Year to you. It is the heartfelt wish of

Y[r]. affectionate

"Little Maiden"

Arthur Sullivan was apparently a very interesting young lover. In one of Louise's letters, Freddie Clay suffers in comparison.

To have loving ways I see requires training like any other quality and I think it ought to be much more largely put into practice because it is a source of so much pleasure. I am sure it is because Freddie has had so little to do with women that he has none. No pretty little sayings, no pretty pet names and I feel quite a stranger with him.

The pet names employed in the Scott Russell family were very important. The girls had childhood names that they used for each other.

LADY	Louise
CHENNIE	Rachel
DICKIE	Alice

With Sullivan's arrival, however, a few more names were created.

LITTLE WOMAN	Sullivan's name for Louise
LITTLE MAIDEN	Sullivan's name for Alice
PASSION FLOWER	Rachel's name for herself
FOND DOVE	Sullivan's name for Rachel
BIRDIE	Rachel's name for Sullivan or herself
LOVING A.	Sullivan's signature to Rachel

But of all the pet names that came into use at the time, the one that took on the most significance was "Fond Dove". This derived from a poem by Jane Ingelow, *O Fair Dove, O Fond Dove*, which Sullivan set to music at Rachel's suggestion. It became the theme song of their romance. "Passion Flower" was abandoned and a great deal of *bird* imagery began to appear in Rachel's letters.

My feathers are all up the wrong way and it will want a great deal of petting, billing and cooing to bring them down again.

A dove, the classical symbol of purity, became Rachel's new identity in her romantic fantasy. When she wasn't Sullivan's dove she was "Bird" or "Birdie".

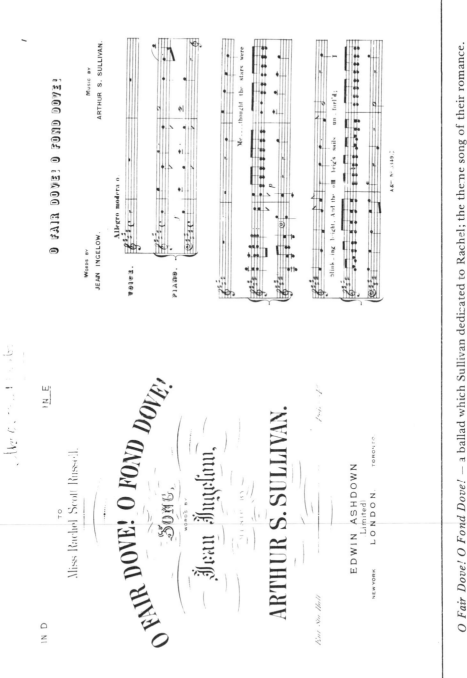

O Fair Dove! O Fond Dove! – a ballad which Sullivan dedicated to Rachel; the theme song of their romance.
(Pierpont Morgan Library)

My blessed darling I am glad to be in your power, glad to be yours to do what you like with. I feel no fear that he will crush the feathers of his tender dove, and therefore she nestles fearlessly on his breast, with those dear sheltering arms round her.

Even Louise began to refer to Rachel as "Birdie" and very shortly the whole family was speaking (and writing letters) in bird talk — an insipid variation of baby talk, inspired by Rachel's relationship.

Oo is an ittle beast — and even if oo knows, birdie certainly does not know what made oo so cross on Saturday. She suppose it was only oo's dwefful temper cropping up!

But as Rachel's clandestine romance was taking on the qualities of passion, guilt and infancy, it was becoming more and more obvious to Mama that poor Harry Wynne had not been working his way into Rachel's affections as she had hoped.

Harry Wynne wants to marry me — and this has been an extra trouble and difficulty to me. Oh Birdie, it is too funny to see them all walking in couples round the garden discussing my affairs — it makes me <u>boil</u> inwardly.

This is the family divided. Papa <u>neutral</u> — a little inclined to the Wynne coalition. Mama an enemy. Dickie an enemy. Lady, a staunch friend. Norman, anti-Wynne — but not for the other!! [i.e., not for Sullivan.] I never speak to anyone about anything as I keep my own counsel and am as firm as a rock.

Rachel took pains to assure Sullivan that she had let her new suitor know exactly how she felt.

Harry Wynne knows <u>quite</u> well I do not love him. If he thinks — rather chooses to imagine otherwise — he is mad as a hatter. I told him that he might as well ask me to love and marry Norman as him — and that I <u>never</u> would care for him in any other way than that. Also, remember this — you are the only man whose love for me does not make me <u>sick</u> — and I was so rude and disagreeable to Harry that not only did Mama speak to me about it — but

58

he himself came and implored me to be womanly in my manner to him. "Only", I said, "remember this — I never can love you — and if I am agreeable and womanly to you, you will be mistaking it for something else and then you will say I behaved badly."

Harry Wynne took the hint and a short time later confessed that from the first time he spoke to Rachel "he felt and knew that it was hopeless". Exit Harry Wynne.

Soon after Harry departed, however, Rachel found herself facing another problem. Her father, who was having difficulty finding engineering commissions in England, was offered a job on the Continent as a consultant to a Swiss ferry company. Rachel had never been in the best of health, and the strain of her uncertain romance had weakened her. Towards the end of July, it was decided that Rachel would spend the autumn months with her father in Switzerland. Rachel would have wanted nothing less than to be hundreds of miles away from Sullivan at a time when she was so unsure of him.

Now tell me this my sweet one, may I leave my love and honour safe in your hands? Will you keep them and cherish them and will you be quite true to me all that long time we do not meet?

———◆———

Remember, it will be hard — for you must give me a spotless life and a pure love — and darling, the future is oh, so hard, so hard. Can you bear it? Mind, I don't ask it. I only pray you on my knees, by your God, by the memory of your father, by all you hold sacred — be noble and good whether I am by to help you or not.

It was arranged that Rachel would spend the entire autumn in Switzerland. She did not dare to tell her parents that she did not want to go, or why. As she thought about leaving England, she wrote to Sullivan with only one request:

Darling, will you do this? I wish you would give me some little thing that I can wear always and that I can send back to you when you have broken your faith — something which, as long as it is with me, will be an outward and visible sign of your faith.

This was a request that Sullivan was happy to fill. Just before Rachel left the country he gave her a ring and it improved her spirits a little.

> *Oh! darling, darling, I can scarcely bear the pain of this separation and the longing feeling I get and the loneliness and the fear that perhaps my darling may change. Surely surely such a thing is not possible after all the words of love and faith that have been spoken. No, darling . . . that little gold ring is the outward and visible sign of our great inward love and if I have it to kiss, and can say to it, "As this little gold band winds round my finger clasping it and making it its own — so my darling has found me round in his love, making me body and soul his."*

Nevertheless, Rachel could not leave the country without addressing a few words to her ideal, fantasy Sullivan.

> *I saw the change in you on Saturday and felt that of us two, you were the truer and the firmer and since then, darling, there is such a quiet feeling of peace in my heart . . .*

And from Switzerland Rachel sent her ideal the following verses:

> *Unless you can love as the Angels may*
> *With the breadth of Heaven betwixt you —*
> *Unless you can dream that his faith is fast*
> *Through knowing and unknowing —*
> *Unless you can die when that dream is past,*
> *Oh! never call it loving.*

In the beginning of September, Rachel and Papa arrived at the resort Allée Saal in Switzerland. It was a charming hotel with pretty public gardens, but Rachel was far from happy there. In the evenings she would see the other girls in the hotel strolling about the grounds with their husbands and gentlemen friends and it only increased her loneliness.

By the end of September Mama joined her and the weather turned cold. "We are the only inmates of this hotel." Rachel wrote. "I feel as if I were on a desert island." Mama stayed a few weeks and then returned to London, and Rachel and

Papa moved on to Zurich. "I don't feel that this place has done me good," Rachel wrote as they left.

There were many guests at the new hotel and a number of eligible young men in Zurich. One of them in fact, the son of a well-to-do Swiss family, became quite captivated by Rachel. His name was François Rausch. But Rachel wanted little to do with him or any other young man she met there. As the winter approached her thoughts were exclusively of Sullivan.

My little bed is turned back all ready for use and oh! how I wish a little curly black head were lying on it and that I might lay mine down beside it.

Back in England, however, Arthur Sullivan's thoughts were not of Rachel. In September and October he went to a large number of parties in London. In November he made a historic trip to Vienna with George Grove where the two of them discovered two lost Schubert symphonies and the *Rosamunde* music. Towards the end of the year Sullivan and Frank Burnand completed a new comic opera, *The Contrabandista*, which opened on 18th December. And so as 1867 came to an end, Sullivan's primary concern was his career in the theatre, not Rachel. He neglected to send her a Christmas present; he did not even send her a Christmas card; and on New Year's Eve Rachel found herself alone in body and soul.

New Years Eve

My darling heart,
It has hurt me unspeakably that you could let Xmas and the New Year pass without a wish or a greeting for the only person whose word could have brought me happiness. It is so sad because it is those little things which show me that I am not always present with you. I feel heartsick and weary tonight and yet I am going home! — In a week perhaps I may see you but how — and where — Oh! I dread it all. I dread that your love may have changed. I dread the cold sick feeling of unsatisfied longing and I am so tired, so tired, and I want so to rest.

61

Two photographs of Rachel taken in Zurich in 1867. On the back of
one she wrote the words *Fest und Treu*. (Pierpont Morgan Library)

Perhaps God is teaching me where alone I must put my love and my trust — not in any man — and if so I must learn — but oh! the lesson will be bitter. I wonder what you have been doing this last week?

I have <u>dreamt</u> of you constantly, such sad dreams — and I have such a foreboding feeling in my heart. Oh! this new year, this new year — which should bring us together. But on all sides I see that there is nothing perfect or lasting and I somehow feel that our beautiful future will have clouds. I dream of our house and of our life and the music within. I see it all so clearly and yet in my heart of hearts something tells me it is all a dream. My own one, when I look in your dear eyes and feel your true firm hand clasping mine — shall I feel faith then? Arthur my dear one you must not try me now — I am not strong and I am still so passionate and I will not stand the pain you gave me before. You must treat poor little bird so tenderly — caress her — carry her in your heart so warm so warm and do not let anything hard or unkind touch her.

I am so frightened darling — have you been spoiling our love? What have you done that I feel this fear and terror? Did you read Artist and Model in "London Poems"? There were such beautiful things in it which suited us — my love and me — lovely things but all a little sad. Everything is tinged with sadness.

Oh! I want to lie in your arms just one night — to feel again that <u>sleep</u> content — that perfect rest.

Arthur dearest I am speaking to you very earnestly now — sitting at your knees — with your hand against my cheek — Darling our future lies more with you than with me — It depends on your love. If it is always with me — unswerving — eternal as rock — if I feel that you cannot live without your bird — that your life is nothing without her — then I can have strength to go through it all — But if I feel you could love anyone else, be happy and satisfied with them — or if I feel your love is not what, thank God, I believe it is — pure good beautiful — a piece of God Himself, His best gift — then darling mine I had rather give it all up — though I think it would break my heart.

Bless you darling. The tears are raining down so fast I cannot see.

Here is the New Year. Dear old year goodbye. We thank you — my darling and I, for we are one — we thank you for all the happiness you have given us — and New Year — we pray you to look kindly on us — bring us two together, dear New Year — if we are worthy.

God bless my darling a thousand times now and always. My darling, can you see the arms held out to you and the brown eyes full of tears — but even with tears they are melting with the love looks for you.

What does my true love answer?

Goodbye, my Heart, goodbye — when you get this, how near we shall be — for on Friday we shall be home.

Arthur, Arthur, my own one love

Your fond fond Dove
Your little bird.

CHAPTER THREE

The Bush Burnt With Fire

(January 1868 — September 1868)

> *... now go to sleep darling mine, and dream of the brown bird who loves you dearly — and who will some day be your own to love and cherish and torment ...*
>
> — Rachel to Sullivan

The Crystal Palace

Rachel was home. The long and lonely autumn months were over. It had been a miserable and anxious time abroad and Rachel had survived it only by thinking continuously about the man whom she had been sent away to forget.

Her absence had changed nothing. She still wanted to marry Sullivan. She was still afraid to tell her parents, and reluctant to be seen with Sullivan in public. All of this was having a wearying effect upon her. "I have lost my youth," she wrote him on 18th January. "You are the only hope of bringing it back. Marry me." But this was easier said than done, for even if Sullivan had been willing to marry Rachel immediately, there were still many problems. During Rachel's five months abroad, Sullivan had not put any money aside for their marriage as he had promised. This meant that Rachel did not dare tell her mother that they were planning to marry soon, and *that* meant that the secret meetings would have to continue. Sullivan disliked them intensely. "I quite think with you about the concealment," Rachel wrote, "only I *will not* tell Mama about it."

> *If you like we will be _friends_, dear friends and friends only with nothing to conceal until you can go to Mama and ask her for me and this is what I should best like and it would prove besides whether your love will really stand.*

Rachel's remark about being "friends only" suggests that there was still another aspect of their relationship that was causing trouble.

> *My sweet one,*
>
> *Your letter made me a little sad, for it showed me that your love could not stand the test of absence and that only physical contact could recreate it into what it was. — Ah me! When I think of those days when cooing and purring was enough for us — till we tried the utmost — and that is why I fancy _marriage_ spoils love. When you can drink _brandy_ water tastes sickly afterwards — and so I feel that mere petting and cooing will have no charm for us any more and that when we satisfy our passion then all those little endearments will cease to have any charm. Do you not fear that too, darling, and that that is the reason why marriage gets so commonplace that people see and have*

so much of each other morally and physically that they get satiated and the freshness of the charm and attraction wears off. Darling, why are you not coming today? Because you had enough of me yesterday, and are quietly contented to wait till another opportunity occurs? When will you come again — Don't you want to see me darling, or can you wait patiently? Ah birdie, birdie, where shall I turn as your love gets cold. It is not the same thing as it was when you saw me daily constantly and I feel as if my heart would break if your love grew cold.

There are no more the same endearments and caresses and tendernesses — if it is not passion, it is nothing — and I do so fear I have given myself to you too completely. You no longer care to see me or be with me unless you can give way to that completely.

Is it not so, Arthur, my own love? And your letters are so short and so different to the long love letters I used to get. I feel inclined to say, "Take me Mother Earth! I have loved and been beloved," but I don't want even to waken from my dream except in Heaven!

'Passion Flower' was becoming a bit more conservative. However, if 'Loving A.' had still not even begun to save his money for their wedding, he was hardly worthy of "the utmost".

But Rachel had been back in England for a month by this time and *nothing* she had said or done had been successful in getting Sullivan to prepare himself for their marriage. Finally, Rachel concluded, that if she really intended to marry him, *she* would have to take the upper hand.

And now Darling, I want you seriously to sit down and consider whether we shall really be able to marry in May. Be practical and sit down and calculate it all quietly without any partiality — including your debts — and the allowance you will make for your mother — (in which your brother ought to share). Then tell me the result darling and we will put our little wise practical heads together and see if it can be done. It is quite a different case to Freddie and Dickie because they will live free of cost, to say nothing of a carriage and horses, and his income will merely be pin money. It is a little trying to think of how very smooth the course of their love is compared to ours! . . .

May God bless you darling — be good and faithful and earnest — you have put your shoulder to the wheel — and self-denial must be used now — you must pay off all your debts — and you must not fritter away your money now — Remember, the possession of your bird depends on the power you have of denying yourself.

Unfortunately Sullivan did not take kindly to Rachel's offer to organize his finances. In fact he resented her presumption and he replied with an angry letter (now lost) in which he apparently informed her that he was quite capable of managing his own life, and that if she objected to the way he managed it, there was certainly no reason for her to continue to play a part in it. Furthermore, Sullivan probably added, if Rachel were so ashamed of him that she couldn't face telling her mother of her plans to marry him, perhaps she should not marry him after all. Once more Rachel became hysterical.

Oh! Arthur Arthur how cruel you are.

I can scarcely write. I am quivering from head to foot with the sick pain of your letter   How could you write to me like that after my letter to you — Oh! I am heartsick and weary, and you are so cold so cold.

My heart's love — the only thing which will give me courage and life — is the warm unchangeable clasp of your dear hand holding me up and the well of pure deep unalterable love in your eyes, the only thing. — Oh! Arthur, surely you owe me something? You came to me when I was happy as the birds on the trees, as bright as a summer day and the light and life of this house, full of health and buoyancy. You came — you crept into my life and my blood. You stole away my love. You have left me — what am I now, and the only thing which will bring them all back, you take away.

Poor little thing — are you as tired? Come and rest your head on the soft breast of your fond Dove — it is always there for you. She is never hard or cruel — always tender and loving even in her letters. The world is so hard and cold that she knows so well if one has not one warm loving place to lay one's head — that one is too sad, and would wish to die. So come darling — lay it there — close the dear eyes — then I kiss them till they feel quite bright — and I stroke the dear curls and kiss them and say love, love — am I all the world to thee? Can I fill it all out for you so that it is quite complete — no want mental or physical — not one your Passion Flower cannot fill. Oh! Darling, my passionately loved one — take me home darling to my house and your house — our home.

I shall not go to the Glehns either tonight. I only went for you. Just to see and speak to you. Darling come to the Palace on Saturday. I will walk and talk and sit with you under everyone's eyes and Mama will then speak to me — and I promise you I will tell her — oh! my sweet, my sweet, be kind to me — Ah, be kind. Do you not count your promises as something — and you said — I never should hear a cruel unkind word from your lips before — and now — the unkindest, almost the only cruel words which were ever said to me have come from you.

My darling, you are sad and bitter and sore. You should not be. I am not changed and I have promised to be your wife. Your very own — whenever and wherever you may choose. It all lies in your hands. Only do not blame me for wishing to save those who brought me into this world — and have loved and treasured me ever since and made me what you love — some unnecessary pain, now when they have so much trouble and bitter sorrow. Mind darling there is no hesitation in my mind, none. I will do it bravely, straightforwardly, as soon as you say to me — "such and such a time I will marry you darling — you must get ready now."

. . . Remember you only won me by the sheer force of your love. And with it alone you can keep me. In that and with it you are my master and I bow to you and do your will — but I must look up and see that eternal unfathomable love shining in your eyes and the tender smile of unalterable love in your face.

70

Sullivan did not reply. A few days later when Rachel had recovered her composure, she wrote to him more calmly and asked him to meet her one day at the Crystal Palace. She wanted to talk things over. Fortunately Sullivan did too and they arranged to see each other the next weekend. When they met, they were both willing to compromise.

A concert in the vast central hall of the Crystal Palace. The auditorium could accommodate as many as three thousand performers and many times that number of listeners. When Sullivan and Rachel met at a concert they were easily lost in the crowd

Sullivan insisted that Rachel tell her mother about him immediately. In return for this, Sullivan said that he would begin to set up house for her — or at least to save a bit of money for the purpose — or at least to try to anyway. This of course was all that Rachel wanted to hear, because she knew that if Sullivan were really willing to save his money, her parents would have no grounds on which to object to him. She was ecstatically happy. Sullivan had reassured her of his love and she was convinced that they would be married that spring.

"Perfect love casteth out fear"

I thought, my darling, that I held in my arms a beautiful flower, beautiful with a more than earthly — a divine beauty — because I dreamed that it was God's own gift to me — and so I loved it and treasured it.

And one day, ah me! — I awoke and saw that tho (sic) *its beauty was great — it was not divine, but of the earth — earthy — and I trembled to know that being of the earth, my beautiful flower must die.*

So I felt when you spoke to me yesterday, and showed me what had seemed to me divine in your love, its steadfastness, its infinity was a dream . . .

I woke up this morning with a sense of loss — and yet I have been so happy all day — happier than I have been for two years, because I have got you back again into my life and I will never let you go again. The old feeling of contented rest has come back again — and contented with your great love — even tho it's not what I dreamed it was . . .

I feel as if a leaden weight had fallen off from me, and as if I could be your bright loving bird again, and that all the tears were gone, and the agony passed through in those few hours on Saturday . . .

I will speak to Mama and tell her quite frankly that you see now that it was a dream and that you do not any more wish to take your little bird home to your nest, but that I have never been happy since you went away, and that I am going to write to you constantly, and if she does not wish you to come here, I shall take every opportunity

*of seeing you quite frankly and openly elsewhere — and
then my darling it is like new life again — all the floodgates
will be opened, and we will be happy so happy together
again.*

And finding herself in exuberant spirits for the first time in
many months, Rachel prepared to speak to her parents.

Mama had to be told now and quickly too because Sullivan
was anxious to announce the engagement, and if word were
to filter back to Mama before Rachel had a chance to explain
things, there would really be trouble. ". . . we are living on
such a volcano," Rachel wrote, "that it may burst anyday
now and scatter us to the four winds."

Rachel knew that when she finally broke the news to her
parents, the reaction would very likely be volcanic, so she
chose to tell them on an evening when her sister Louise was
away with the Glehns. Then, as calmly as possible Rachel
took Mama and Papa aside and explained that she and
Sullivan had never stopped seeing each other even though it
had been forbidden. At this report Mama was greatly disturbed. Rachel added that she and Sullivan were still very
much in love, and that it was their intention to marry in the
spring. Mama could not believe her ears. Rachel also confessed that Louise, Alice, Freddie Clay and a few others had
known about the secret meetings and the engagement all
along. This was too much.

Eight months before Mama had shrieked, "I will sooner
die than let you marry him." She felt as if she had been
betrayed by her own children and nothing, *nothing* would
calm her.

"I have cried as though I were a lake of tears since ten
o'clock last night," Rachel wrote to Sullivan the next day.
"I should like best to lie down quietly and die. My poor
mother lay all night sobbing her heart out, and her dear
face is quite changed."

Louise, however, was relieved that her mother finally
knew the truth and she wrote:

73

It is all over. The terrible words have been spoken. O the relief. No more hiding, no more deception. I was staying with the Glehns so knew nothing till this morning when Birdie came to tell me. It was very brave of her because we all know how terrible it would be. However much is better than we expected. Papa is an angel. There never was nor could be anybody the least like him and so you see he is our prop and comfort which was what we never dared hope. The rest we can bear. Any certainty can be borne. Birdie feels the worst is over and a sort of peace following the most troubled months of existence . . . Never again, please God.

So Rachel had the support of one parent at least. She wrote:

Papa says we must either marry <u>now</u> or it must be broken off altogether, for it is quite impossible for us to go on living like this, or indeed for me to live with my mother for a long time to come.

Papa had just been with Rachel for five long and lonely months abroad. He knew how deep her feelings for Sullivan ran. Now he was telling her that if she truly loved him she must marry him immediately — as he was. There was no reason to expect him to change.

But this was not acceptable to Rachel, for she knew that if she were to marry Sullivan now, she would have to move into his three bachelor rooms in Pimlico, where she and heaven knows who else had been with him. She would also have to accept that Mama would probably not go to the wedding, and even with her father's support, the best that life could offer was the man she loved and very little money. In her present state of mind she could not accept it.

. . . I want a time of quiet and peace after all this dreadful business — to know my own mind truly and clearly. Mind, my heart, I don't doubt that I love you — you and no other — but marriage is either heaven or the other thing — and if I were hurried into it like this, I don't know what might happen.

If they had let you come to the house quietly I should have known better what I was doing but with this misery and hardness here, and those restless meetings here and there and anywhere I feel as though I were scarcely my own self.

After this new upheaval she arranged to meet Sullivan at the Crystal Palace and once again he assured her of his love. He reaffirmed the engagement. He promised that they would be married in the spring, and from Rachel's next letter, it appears that Sullivan gave her much needed reassurance on another subject as well.

I won't ever be afraid of "that thing" again. I know well you would not have loved me so well if I had not that physical power over you too — only it frightens me a little sometimes — for fear that when you have got me body and soul you will care too much for the former. I am not afraid now and will not be again. I know your love would not be what it is without it — and as it is — so it is perfect to me.

One magic day together and all was well. Once more it appeared that everything was settled; Rachel would only have to wait for Sullivan and the spring.

The winter, however, was not promising to be easy. Louise was the only friend that Rachel had in Westwood Lodge. Papa, her greatest ally, was still spending much of his time on the Continent on business, and Mama was still smarting from her "betrayal".

To make matters more complicated, Frank Rausch, who had become captivated with Rachel in Switzerland, had followed her back to England. Rachel was not interested in his attentions. Mama of course would have been aware of the fact that Rausch was from a very fine Swiss family and Rachel's indifference to him could only have added to her frustration. Mrs Scott Russell was making life very difficult for her daughters that winter and Rachel complained about it frequently:

I think her behaviour is very cruel, but I suppose she looks upon my past conduct as worse and unpardonable and treats me accordingly. I feel inclined to say, "My punishment is more than I can bear" and it is more than I can bear cheerfully.

Sullivan may have been the cause of Mama's ill humour and Mama may have succeeded in banning him from the house, but she had not succeeded in keeping him out of her family's thoughts.

Two such comic things happened today. First Mama asked Lady who a certain book was written by and Lady said without thinking, "Mr. Sullivan"!!! And at dinner Papa said to Fred, "Hand it to me, Sullivan" — I nearly went off into an explosion and buried my head in my plate. It showed where the thoughts of the family were wandering to.

Much of the time, however, Rachel found herself the object of considerable resentment within the family — especially as the winter wore on and Alice began to have problems of her own with Freddie Clay.

Then followed some argument, I forget what, about composers and Mama said: "Of course we cannot judge because we don't know any really good or great composers," and Dickie chimed in, "No we don't."

I daresay you can guess how these things hurt when I remember when, one short year ago, you were down here the favoured of all and more welcome than anyone before or since.

All of this family tension of course would have been bearable if Arthur Sullivan had merely been true to the promises he had made in February. But he was not. As the weeks went by it was growing more and more obvious that he was doing nothing to prepare himself for marriage in the spring and Rachel was becoming very concerned.

It makes me so angry. It is simply stupid and ridiculous and such mere self-indulgence and it is a mere excuse for not doing any work.

If I were a man and loved a girl and that my possessing her depended entirely on my work and energy, I would strain every nerve . . . But I don't think men can love now-a-days — or else they sit still and expect the apples to drop in their mouths.

76

Rachel was angry because Sullivan's behaviour was not making sense. His interest in her appeared to be suddenly waning. He wrote to her less and less. He saw her seldom, and when he did see her he was frequently rude. It was almost as if Rachel's worst fear was coming true: that as a result of giving herself to Sullivan too completely he no longer cared for her as he once had. *But how could this be happening?* Hadn't the two of them sorted everything out? Apparently not. Sullivan's attitude towards Rachel seemed to swing on a pendulum from great intimacy to great hostility. Now it seemed to be swinging towards hostility.

Throughout the winter and spring Rachel's letters give a running account of Sullivan's discourtesies. The last week in February he arranged to meet her at the Crystal Palace reading room, but never appeared. In the beginning of March he spoke unkindly of Mama. At the end of the month Rachel complained to him for not writing to her, and he rewarded her with an "icy" letter. On 2nd April she asked why he had suggested meeting her in George Grove's office knowing Grove was away. A few days later she was upset to learn that Sullivan had been announcing in London that he was engaged to her one day and saying that the engagement was off the next.

But in spite of Sullivan's misbehaviour Rachel could not deny her love for him:

My darling one — Oh! Arthur I want *you, I* want *you — it is the old cry, always the same, my love — the cavern is there, the inner solitude which only one presence can fill.*

———◆———

Oh! how I longed for you! — Caroline went to your house to see you and tell you to come to see me in the field near the haystack and I lay there for two hours longing and aching for you — yet feeling all the time you would not come.

Still Sullivan's rudeness persisted as Rachel became more and more desperate. On 23rd April he sent her a cruel note. "I cried so during the symphony," she wrote, "that I thought

I would not sit it out and I dared not stay for *my* song." In her next letter she complained that Sullivan had not said hello to her father the day before. On 1st May she was upset he had spoken angrily to her, and she begged him to visit her the next day for a reconciliation, but by that time she could see the writing on the wall.

Oh! my darling, in the watches of the night those words of yours come back to me ringing in my ears, "How shall I tell you when I do not love you?" Why did you say them?

The unfortunate truth of the matter was that now that the marriage had been positively agreed upon, its approach had begun to fill Sullivan — and Rachel as well — with trepidation. They were *both* unsure of each other. Freddie Clay had once spoken quite frankly to Rachel about Sullivan. "As a rule," he had warned her, "I should not fancy he were given to matrimony. Indeed, I suppose the mere mention of such a thing would send him into hysterics!" Geroge Grove had also warned Rachel that he thought that Sullivan "did not know what 'devotion' meant." And Sullivan himself had once said to Rachel, "Why should we look for perfect love on both sides? It rarely comes." None of these were good prognostications for their wedding.

A short time later Louise summed up Sullivan's attitude with singular accuracy:

You told me the other day your arrangement [with Rachel] *was never to marry but to wait patiently for one another. I think you overrate your own strength to bear a certain truth and would wish the uncertainty back again.*

May or June had been the time that Rachel had once planned for her wedding, but under the circumstances she had no choice but to postpone the date again — and she did so with a considerable amount of guilt.

Forgive me for all the pain I give you — and oh! don't say the idol is shattered because if that be true it can never, in all time to come, be the same again.
I see, darling, that it is all my own fault — and that I have not lived up to my own self or to the ideal you had of me.

Rachel knew that Sullivan was slipping away from her and she did not have the slightest idea what to do about it.

Forgive me, heart's treasure — Arthur, darling, forgive me — I will not give you any more pain. I will go to you in the autumn, darling . . .

Rachel's promise about the autumn may well have been addressed to her "fantasy" Sullivan, for under the circumstances an autumn wedding with the *real* Sullivan was hardly likely.

At the end of July John Scott Russell returned to Westwood from the Continent. Rachel was very confused about the future.

I write for you to decide for me what you wish me to do. Papa has come home and goes back again in ten days. Shall I go, darling?

Sullivan told her to go. Unfortunately, having asked his advice, Rachel felt obliged to take it. From the letters that follow it appears as if Rachel had asked Sullivan whether she should go in the hope that he would have told her to stay.

I feel going away terribly as is natural, feel putting the Sea between me and my love. Only we "can love as the angels may with the breadth of Heaven betwixt us," and I leave with calm eternal faith and trust in your changeless love — my precious one.
. . . Darling I wish I could give you everything beautiful and priceless in the world — and I have given you all I had to give — myself and my endless tender passionate love.

———◆———

I know only too well what the dreadful yearning and craving to see you will become unless I have the certainty of seeing you . . .
I am in such a nervous fearful state — I wake up at night and in the morning with that terrified dread in my heart of something dreadful having happened.

———◆———

I do so long to see you . . . My sweet one — it seems such ages since we met and I am going away so soon — Arthur, Arthur can you resist it?

———◆———

If you don't write to me I shall consider you are tired of it all and wish to give it up. God help me. If there was one thing I trusted in, it was your undying love — and now a few weeks — and it is all gone. I feel simply heartbroken. Triumph in the thought of that if you like — and the way in which you have wrecked my beautiful bright young life. Is it Good-bye forever?

And on that note Rachel left the country. As soon as she was gone, Freddie Clay decided that it was time for him to step out of the Scott Russell family. It was almost as if the two romances were linked.

But Freddie was timid and he lacked the courage to speak to Alice himself. Instead he announced in London that he was breaking off the engagement and allowed this information to be carried back to Sydenham by friends and neighbours. When Alice learned by report that her engagement had been broken off, she was furious. When Freddie heard how upset she was, he added insult to injury by saying that he had "only promised to marry her because she was so in love with him."

Alice, however, had *many* admirers. One of them was Frank Rausch who by this time had given up hope on Rachel. Alice began to see Rausch, among others, for she was determined not to pine for Freddie Clay as she had seen Rachel pine for Sullivan.

While all of this was taking place in Sydenham, Rachel wrote rather transparently to Sullivan from Switzerland:

I dreamt last night that Freddie had talked you into not loving me and I was so glad when I woke and knew that no-one could change your love. Darling, I glory in it so, and I have such faith in it and you . . .

Tell me what you are doing and thinking and what you think Freddie and Dickie are up to.

When Rachel found out what Freddie had actually been up to she became furious, and she wrote (ungrammatically) to Sullivan: "You cannot both be engaged to me and Freddie's friend." Shortly thereafter, however, she received a letter from Sullivan to say that he was coming to visit her in Switzerland, and somehow she forgot her indignation.

But Sullivan was not going to Switzerland for a social visit. When he arrived there he quickly informed Rachel of his purpose. It was obvious that their engagement was not working — Rachel's mere presence in Switzerland was confirmation of that — and he felt that the two of them ought to look upon the time that Rachel was spending there as a sort of trial separation. As long as she was away, there was to be *no further communication* between them. They could reconsider their feelings for each other when she returned. Rachel was horrified, but Sullivan insisted. Freddie Clay had chosen the cowardly way out. Sullivan was using direct confrontation. Rachel cried, and Sullivan returned quietly to London. He had begun to end it.

Once Sullivan had gone, Rachel felt more alone than ever. She had spent most of her engagement linked to her fiancé by letter. She could not bear this last fragile tie to be broken, and after a little while, she began to write to him again. But once more it was the fantasy Sullivan to whom she was writing:

My treasured one, we will try so hard to be worthy — each of the other — worthy of the best — highest part, each of each — and when we come together, Oh! my love — it will be such perfect happiness.

———◆———

My faith is perfect. If your love could change — then I could believe in no love, in no faithfulness . . . You are my God's gift — and your love for me is God's gift to you.

———◆———

Though we are not near, still, darling, in spirit we are close together. Nothing can separate our souls now. Still in the darkness we can feel the other's hand guiding, helping onwards.

Perhaps, deep down, Rachel already knew that she had lost him. But if she did, knowing the truth only made her cling to her fantasy all the more. Sullivan had worked his way into every aspect of her being. Sullivan was her dream, her reality, her career, and her future all rolled into one. If she had to give him up, she would have an unlivable life ahead.

Unfortunately, it is necessary to have something before you can part with it, and Sullivan's love was something that Rachel, except in fantasy, had never completely had. Their union had never been total because Sullivan had never been prepared to make it so, and Rachel had never been willing to accept anything less.

This was the reason why, in the last analysis, it was so very difficult for Rachel to let Arthur Sullivan go. This was why she would continue to dream about his love for a long, long time — because she had never really possessed it. Her dream had been and always would be just a dream. During her romance, during her estrangement, and all throughout her engagement, Rachel had lived in a world of fantasies and ideals, which corresponded only fleetingly to the actual behaviour of her lover. All this time Rachel had been able to fulfil herself merely in her correspondence. Only in her letters had she been able to create and dwell, with little fear of contradiction from reality, in the private world of fantasy that she preferred. And now, even the letters would stop.

On the back of the envelope of one of the last letters that Rachel wrote to Sullivan in 1868 she scribbled a few words from the Old Testament, words which could well have summed up her life:

> *And the bush burnt with fire*
> *but the bush was not consumed.*

CHAPTER FOUR
Enter Louise

(September 1868 — December 1868)

Shall I go and see you to-morrow? Do you think I may? There could be no harm. You are so nearly my brother . . .
— Louise to Sullivan

Louise Scott Russell

The Scott Russells were a closely-knit family, and the girls, from the moment they first experienced romance, felt that they had to be in love (in one way or another) every single moment. Even Louise, who never had any romantic interest of her own, appeared perfectly content to experience the joy and pain of loving Arthur Sullivan through her sister Rachel. Louise's *true* feelings for Sullivan, however, ran somewhat deeper.

Louise wrote to Sullivan a number of times in 1867 and 1868. It was of course on sister Rachel's behalf that Louise began her correspondence with Sullivan. Nevertheless, she managed to make her own feelings for him quite clear.

> *I don't like you to have headaches and look worn. Are you love-sick? Shall you never be better till you have a bird for quite your own? . . . Shall I go and see you tomorrow? Do you think I may? There could be no harm. You are so nearly my brother . . .*

———◆———

> *I should like to break through all the rules, give vent to all the pent up affection of months, but* à quoi bon! *I do long ineffably to see you.*

In 1864 Louise, aged twenty-three, had written, "My feelings fight with my propriety". By the age of twenty-seven, however, she was ready to "break through all the rules", and as it happened, circumstances were suddenly combining to allow her to do so.

Rachel had gone to Switzerland at the end of July (1868) with her father. Her mother joined them for a few weeks in September, and this left nobody at home with Louise and Alice. Alice, who had just finished with Freddie Clay, took advantage of her parents' absence to burst back onto the social scene. This reaction set an interesting example for the generally reserved Louise. She thought about Sullivan in London. Rachel, Mama and Papa were all away which left Sullivan temptingly alone in Claverton Terrace. All of this freedom was too much to resist. Love knows no loyalties, apparently, not even among sisters.

Enter Louise.

Rachel had left England in August, and Louise and Sullivan probably started seeing each other sometime in September. From the evidence that survives it is reasonable to assume that the new relationship began in this way.

Louise had told Sullivan that she felt nearly like his sister, although her true feelings were really very different. Sullivan was obviously aware of how she felt. (He had after all flirted with more than one sister in the same family years before in Leipzig.) Given the current strained relationship that existed between Rachel and Sullivan, it was almost inevitable that, in Rachel's absence, Sullivan and Louise would see more of each other. As Louise's parents were away, it was relatively simple for her to leave Westwood when she liked, and meet Sullivan in London. There, for the first time, she would have encountered the 'other Sullivan': the gambler, the spendthrift, the playboy. At the sight of this, of course, Louise was shocked — or at least she assumed she should be.

"I meet with temptation daily in London", Sullivan had told Rachel the year before. Now he told Louise the same thing and Louise realized that she had a mission. If Sullivan's morality was being compromised regularly in London she would have to do something about it, for Sullivan was going to marry her sister. Louise, therefore, decided that she would reform him for Rachel's sake! Given the true nature of Louise's feelings this reasoning was very convenient: it permitted her own relationship with Arthur Sullivan to become as intimate as she liked, because all of her intimacy was being pursued in the interest of 'reforming' him — for her sister. To this end she began to meet Sullivan at his new rooms in Claverton Terrace, and there she began to lecture him about his behaviour — Louise had not been Harriette Scott Russell's daughter for nothing. She would ask him whether he had yielded to temptation since her last visit. Sullivan would wring his hands and bemoan his own weakness (as he had so often done with Rachel) and Louise would beg him to be strong.

As the autumn wore on, Louise's little lectures became cozier and cozier, as Sullivan no doubt portrayed himself as the drifting soul, torn between his fading love for Rachel and his 'temptations' in London. In relation to this, Louise saw herself in contemporary literary terms:

Did you read what Trollope calls a curious fact? That men wanting sympathy in a love affair, though they can never care for any woman again, like the Comforter to be pretty, to have bright eyes and soft little hands, etc., etc. Do you think it is true?

Whatever Sullivan may have thought, even the dedication of Trollope's Comforter could be tried if her efforts proved to be ineffective. And if Sullivan had shown little inclination to abandon his night life for Rachel, he was hardly likely to do so for Louise. This presented Louise with a serious problem: if Sullivan did not reform — at least a little — before Rachel returned, the entire justification for seeing him would collapse. "Oh Arthur", she wrote in despair one day, "if you are not good, then I cannot see you. That I know would be wrong", and in this vein she expressed herself in the first letter that survives from this period.

Dearest Arthur,

I am unhappy at thinking you should be tempted not to be good. I cannot bear that you should ever be with anyone who is not nice, or that it could be said, "he is just like other men". Oh Darling, don't touch pitch, don't even look at it. Put away from you what is unlovely and do not desecrate the sacred and beautiful expression of love. You owe it to your future wife during this time of probation to strive to become a man she may trust in and look up to. We come to you so pure and chaste. Why should you think it of little moment that the life of those we call our lord and master should bear so little daylight.

I can forgive it a little where the man's affections are free and where he likes to amuse himself, but you have your love and your little woman to fill up the blank. When we have a love, we carry him in our hearts and he keeps us strong and faithful. Why is it not so with you?

I can offer not the slightest reward for good behaviour because you have taken as your right the only thing I have to give, but I can try to be even more tender and loving and pray "that he may be kept from temptation and made strong and good". Good night and God bless you.

> *Your own devoted*
> *Little Woman*

Unfortunately, this was exactly the type of moralizing that Sullivan despised, and Louise should have known it. He replied with a furious letter in which he justified his own behaviour. "What's the use of resisting!" he wrote callously and then attacked Louise's attitude towards him. Sullivan wrote:

> *The superiority which <u>some</u> women assume over men is very odd. When women take up their parable and censure men for things they do — not understanding how or why it has come about that they have done them — they are in the position of superior beings talking unmitigated rubbish!*

Could Sullivan have been serious when he wrote this? Didn't he realize that Louise's 'crusade' was her only justification for seeing him? Louise responded with a letter that was disturbingly reminiscent of Rachel's.

Dearest Arthur —

> *I have read your letter over and over again trying to find one word of comfort in vain. It all brings nothing but pain, sickening pain. It was best you should write it as you felt it, but that you could write it and that is true. Why did you say you loved me, why did you tell me I kept you good and made you happier — was it that I might feel the more, knowing I had failed?*
>
> *"What's the use of resisting?" Have you ever thought of what the world would be if we never resisted? Have we implanted in us the intense love for all that is beautiful and good all for nothing and were we not sent a bright and shining example in whom there was no guile that we might follow after Him? Could you bear other men to look upon you as you look on those of them who have not resisted? Oh, Arthur, I know I have no right to say all this. I know that through us all this misery has been brought upon you . . .*

Is there no help? Will you not even try to put it all behind you? Could you not throw yourself into your work, go only to see nice people, and try to believe that all will come right? Oh, Arthur, if you are not good I cannot see you, that I <u>know</u> would be wrong — besides, where would be the good.

Oh, my darling, if you love me a little, do not take it from me. I have had such a sinless life. Circumstances I can bear, but if of your own free will you chose to give me up I should yearn after the place where there is no sin, where all our tears shall be dried up and where there will be perfect peace and perhaps it might please God to take me.

> *ever your own*
> *Little Woman*

Somehow Sullivan was moved by Louise's gripping appeal, and he made a point of seeing her the next day. Sullivan had often reassured Rachel after he had upset her. This time he reassured her sister. He told her that he was not as unrepentant as she believed, and that her "lectures were doing some good". Louise was much relieved at this news because it would justify her continuing to see him.

I felt so much happier last night after having seen you and carried your sweet little letter about me . . .

I can't think now how I could believe anything evil of you even though you yourself tried to convince me. Now when you say it I shall only believe that you are unhappy and though you cannot know how gladly I would take your burden from you and bear it so that <u>you</u> might not suffer, still it is not the hopeless feeling that you are not what I love.

Nevertheless, Louise still felt a certain amount of guilt about her relationship with Sullivan.

Oh, if only I knew whether it is quite and decidedly wrong to love you so, but you won't tell me and yet I am sure you know. When I am sentenced to that warm place shall you come and say, "it was partly my fault?"

Louise was beginning to have second thoughts about her relationship with Sullivan. At the same time her sister Alice, now free from her engagement to Freddie Clay, was enjoying sudden popularity with the young men of Sydenham. Louise, curiously, was not even jealous.

Oh to be watched and followed and thought of and petted, and the rest of the world to be as nothing and the woman to know she can make that man's life bright and happy. However I did not feel at all lonely. I thought, I am his little woman and I don't care.

Sullivan sent her a kind letter in answer to this, and Louise replied:

You have taken my position for a little, so now you can know how sweet it is to feel you can comfort and bring sunshine and happiness into another life. You see, I can not judge as to whether I like other people's petting because I have no experience . . .

But Louise, not unreasonably, had begun to have doubts about the propriety of obtaining her experience from Arthur Sullivan.

Suppose we arrange not to meet at all till it becomes an absolute necessity, and then suppose we say there is to be no petting. Would you like that? We could talk and be near one another and enjoy each other's society; would it be nice? Or is there really only one thing that makes one thoroughly comfy and warm? Oh how sad and that that one thing should be wicked, though I can't find any passage in the Bible where it is forbidden or even alluded to, so perhaps if they take no notice of it, we need not!

———◆———

I suppose you don't want to see her this week because you are so strong and good. "Little woman need not apply. No petting required!" She ought to be glad because it shows her little lectures have done good. Only I don't like not to know for a day how you are, what thinking, what feeling and that I know best when I am quite close beside 'oo, only I would rather wait till 'oo feels a great want.

By the end of the year it would appear that Louise had become so confused about her relationship that her letters were practically carbon copies of Rachel's.

Louise to Sullivan	Rachel to Sullivan
I have read your letter over and over again trying to find one word of comfort in vain. It all brings nothing but pain, sickening pain.	*I can scarcely write. I am quivering from head to foot with the sick pain of your letter — How could you write to me like that . . .*
Do write to me a very sweet and tender letter . . .	*Oh do write to me — a letter to help me and comfort me and warm me . . .*
Oh please don't be very low, don't suffer so much.	*Tell me something of your self and your life. Oh! don't suffer too much. I cannot bear to think of you suffering as I do.*
Oh my darling, I can't write any more because the pain chokes so.	*Bless you darling. The tears are raining down so fast I cannot see.*
One little question: oo does not tiss any but oo's own little woman, does oo?	*Oo is an ittle beast — and even if oo knows, birdie certainly does not know what made oo so cross on Saturday.*

In only a few short months Louise had succeeded in entangling herself in exactly the same web that she had watched Sullivan and her sister take four years to spin.

But Rachel was about to return now and all of a sudden 'Lady' realized how awkward it would be if 'Little Woman' were still involved with 'Loving A.' when 'Fond Dove' came home from Switzerland. "My greatest wish," Louise wrote to Sullivan, "is . . . that you should marry Chennie."

I feel as if she ought to know because I know she cannot realize it and if all were to come right, could you bear to say to her or to feel, "I was utterly unworthy of you?" What is to be done?

What was to be done, indeed? Only one thing. Louise realized that she would have to bring her relationship with Sullivan to an end well before Rachel's return. As it happened, this was easier than she might have expected. One day towards the end of the year Sullivan told Louise that he was *still* seeing other women, and that he would continue to see them. Louise's whole house of cards collapsed.

Dearest Arthur,

So you see it was good-bye after all. I don't know why you wrote me that letter or why you told me that terrible thing except perhaps to try my love. You could not conceive what I have suffered since last night because habit takes the edge off everything and therefore could not realize the awful shock. I would have given years of my life for you to say it was not true. I know of these things of course but never came in direct contact with them before.

If every creature I love had thrown me over I would have stuck to you for ever if I could have helped you to be good. But Arthur <u>can</u> I give part of my life, all that is purest and most sacred in me, lavish on you the first man I ever touched, all that I have of tenderness and feel that to you it can only be a passing fancy? Ought one to sow the seeds of one's own eternal suffering for nothing? I would <u>gladly</u> if I could raise and strengthen you and stamp out all that was wrong when the time came.

Don't let this make you bitter, don't say all women are alike. I think you will miss me a little at first because I have loved you so dearly and I shall pass again through the valley of the shadow.

You need never fear for the <u>least</u> <u>thing</u> you ever told me, it is as safe as though it were buried. I would not hurt you dear, and I shall always try to win for you that which I believe would save you and make you happy. Oh Arthur on my knees I beg of you just try for a little to put it all

(simply odious blotting-paper)

Dearest Arthur —
So you see it was good-bye after all.
I dont know why you wrote me that
letter or why you told me that terrible
thing, except perhaps to try my love.
You could not conceive what I have
suffered since last night because habit
takes the edge off everything & therefore
could not realize the awful shock.
I would have given years of my life
for you to say it was not true. I know
of these things of course but never came
in direct contact with them before.

'So you see it was good-bye after all . . .'. Louise's letter of farewell to
Sullivan, December 1868 (see page 92). (Pierpont Morgan Library)

If every creature I love had thrown me over I would have stuck to you for ever if I could have helped you to be good. But Arthur <u>can</u>. I give part of my life, all that is purest & most sacred in me, lavish on you, the first man I ever touched, all that I have of tenderness & feel that to you it can only be a passing fancy. ought one to sow the seeds of one's own eternal suffering for nothing? I would <u>gladly</u> if I could raise & strengthen you, & stamp out all that was wrong when the time came.

Dont let this make you bitter. dont say all women are alike. I think you will miss me a little at first

because I have loved you so dearly.
& I shall pass again through the valley
of the shadow.
You need never fear for the least thing
you ever told me, it is as safe as though
it were buried. I would not hurt you
dear. & I shall always try to win for
you that which I believe would save
you & make you happy. Oh Arthur on
my knees I beg of you just try for a
little to put it all behind you. I know
it grows & grows till you have no power to save yourself. I feel that I can
not judge of the temptations because
now I know my nature is cold but
surely it must be possible to overcome
it. Don't please take this lightly as

a foolish whim. It must be so because
it is right & best. Dont think her hard,
without. it life will be bitter, not
sweet, bitter but still to be borne.
Oh my darling I can't write any more
because the pain chokes so.
Many will have loved you more
ardently & more passionately but
none could have loved you
more truly & tenderly
than
your own
Little woman.

behind you. I know it grows and grows till you have no power to save yourself. I feel that I can not judge of the temptations because now I know my nature is cold but surely it must be possible to overcome it. Don't <u>please</u> take this lightly as a foolish whim. It <u>must</u> be so because it is right and best. Don't think her hard. Without it life will be bitter, not sweet, bitter, but still to be borne. Oh my darling, I can't write any more because the pain chokes me so. Many will have loved you more ardently and more passionately, but none could have loved you more truly and tenderly than

your own

Little Woman.

Exit Louise.

CHAPTER FIVE

The End Of Guinevere

(January 1869 – June 1870)

> *It is such divine weather and*
> *all the young green things are*
> *budding forth, and I am so sad,*
> *so sad I could lie down on my*
> *"mother earth" — and cry my*
> *heart out.*
>
> — Rachel to Sullivan

Another photograph of Sullivan in the 1860s

The winter of 1868 must have been the all time low for the Scott Russell girls.

Louise had just finished with Sullivan, Alice was recovering from the loss of Freddie Clay, and Sullivan was preparing to break up with Rachel once and for all. Rachel, of course, was still in Switzerland, but she would be returning soon. Therefore, towards the end of January, Sullivan crossed the Channel, and met her unexpectedly in Zurich. Rachel had not known that he was coming or why. But when he arrived he wasted no time in telling her. He took her up to her room and explained that they must not go on seeing each other. Their romance was over. It had in fact ended months ago.

Months ago . . . surely Rachel knew this; but she had never been able to accept it. Now she had no choice. Sullivan was forcing her to face the truth.

"The day of that bitter parting," Rachel wrote eight months later, "the tears that streamed over your poor dove's face were the heralds of oceans of others that were to follow." She could delude herself no longer. Arthur Sullivan was saying goodbye. She cried and he returned to London — again.

Then she stretch'd out her arms and cried aloud,
"O Arthur!" there her voice brake suddenly . . .

I must not scorn myself; he loves me still.
Let no-one dream but that he loves me still.

Tennyson's description of Guinevere's grief at the loss of King Arthur could not have been more apt.

A few days later Rachel gathered all her strength and wrote:

Feb. 3, 69

When you see this ring — you will know that what I write to say now is "Goodbye".

It can have no other ending even in the far future, and your young life shall not be dimmed by the nurture of a hope which will never be fulfilled.

I should have said or written this when you left but my courage failed — I was too cowardly to do it — now that I am going home I must know that all the past is cut off as if it were dead — the dead spring and summer of our

Feb. 3rd/
/69.

When you see this ring – you will know
that what I write to say now is "Goodbye".

It can have no other ending even
in the far future – & your young life
shall not be dimmed by the nurture
of a hope which will never be fulfilled

I should have said or written this
when you left – but my courage failed –
I was too cowardly to do it – now that
I am going home – I must know that all
the past is cut off – as if it were dead –
the dead spring & summer of our lives
as indeed it is. – I hear you are
changed & ill – God help you – &
give you strength & courage to bear it
all. – You have others to work for &
your beautiful genius to live for – & I –
nor any other woman on gods earth – is
worth wasting ones life for. –

I too am changed – so cold – so dead –
you called all the warmth within – &

with you it took wings & fled.

I don't much care what comes now provided I have strength to live well nobly — & to help others in their toil — & you must do the same — only the circle in which you work — is far greater than mine. —

I cannot write — surely you will know & feel all I would say — & all the bitter regret I have for the past. — One never can know or tell what consequences — how bitter how endless — may ensue from a tiny beginning of wrong. — With all my heart I thank you for the past — which has given a color to my life which nothing in the future can change. And I pray God day & night to forgive me for all the misery I have caused you & to turn it to your good & to give you great happiness still —

God bless & keep you pure & noble & good & may He give you strength & comfort.

Rachel Elliott Russell —

'When you see this ring you will know that what I write to say now is "Goodbye"...'. Rachel's letter of farewell to Sullivan, February 1869.
(Pierpont Morgan Library)

lives as indeed it is — I hear you are changed and ill — God help you and give you strength and courage to bear it all. You have others to work for and your beautiful genius to live for, and I — nor any other woman on God's earth is worth wasting one's life for.

I too am changed — so cold — so dead — you called all the warmth into me — and with you it took wings and fled.

I don't much care what comes now provided I have strength to live well and nobly — and to help others in their toil — and you must do the same — only the circle in which you work is far greater than mine.

I cannot write — surely you will know and feel all I would say — all the bitter regret I have for the past. One never can know or tell what consequences — how bitter how endless, may ensue from a tiny beginning of wrong. With all my heart I thank you for the past — which has given colour to my life which nothing in the future can change. And I pray God day and night to forgive me for all the misery I have caused you and to turn it to your good and to give you great happiness still.

God bless and keep you pure and noble and good and only He gives you strength and comfort.

Rachel Scott Russell

This letter was not like the others. It was not written in the heat of passion. It was thorough and deliberate and carefully copied out (see pages 102-3). And it was signed *Rachel Scott Russell* — the only letter to which Rachel had signed her name since her love began. 'Fond Dove' was dead; 'Passion Flower' was dead; and Rachel was Rachel once again, as she had been before she had known Sullivan.

Rachel now saw herself as a martyr to love. She identified more strongly than ever with Guinevere and the way in which Tennyson's heroine had bidden farewell to Arthur the King. So too was Rachel saying goodbye to *her* Arthur, carefully indicating the role which they must follow, "to live well and nobly — and to help others in their toil" or, like Guinevere,

And so wear out in alms-deed and in prayer
The sombre close of that voluptuous day.

This is how lovers behaved at the end of their novels. This is how Rachel Scott Russell ended her love affair.

But while Rachel was playing out her personal tragedy, Alice was adopting an entirely different attitude towards romance. She had lost one man, but would find another, preferably rich. Alice's personality had not been tied to Freddie Clay's — as Rachel's was to Sullivan's — and for that reason she was having little difficulty in finding a replacement.

Not long after she began going out with some of her other young admirers, one of them began to take her fancy — a certain Mr Baxter — and the other young men were (temporarily) dropped. Alice bade them a collective farewell. "Tomorrow," Louise wrote to Sullivan, "some of the boys that Dickie has ruined dine here." Alice in her new role as social butterfly had allowed herself to be seen in public with a number of young men and people were beginning to talk. "I would give worlds," Louise complained, "for Dickie to be married before our reputation is utterly ruined . . ." (Louise of course had not been particularly concerned about her own reputation during the course of her relationship with Sulliven the month before.)

Louise, however, was not the only person who was taking exception to Alice's behaviour. Freddie Clay was not happy to see how well his ex-fiancée was getting on without him, and he expressed his annoyance by writing a letter about some of Alice's recent behaviour to a mutual friend. The letter fell into the hands of Mama. (Life was not kind to Mrs Scott Russell.)

"Mama and I spent a very wretched evening." Louise wrote, "That such a letter *could* be written of one of her daughters nearly kills her, particularly as she realizes that some part of it must be true."

That weekend Alice confronted the less than honourable Freddie Clay and tried to clear the air. All bitterness between them had to end. The past, they agreed, was past. No further letters or remarks would be passed on to third parties, and any residual feelings which Alice and Freddie might still have for each other, whether good or bad, would never be

expressed. The foursome which had begun in days of inno-
cence, and which had occupied the romantic lives of all three
sisters for over five years through youth, joy and pain had
come to an inauspicious end.

And before the year was over, Alice was engaged once
more, to Mr Baxter. Louise, of course, was jealous that her
sister could have found happiness again so soon. But Mama
probably saw things differently. With Papa having to spend
so much of his time working in Switzerland, Mama had
become somewhat sensitive about the finances of the Scott
Russell family, and it would have been a considerable relief
to her to have seen her daughters comfortably married that
year. At one point she even said as much to Louise. "Mama
says I have *such a cold heart* because I won't provide for
myself in the way she thinks fit," Louise wrote.

> *When your parents' love is so far gone that they merely*
> *wish you well provided for, you have no business to*
> *remain a burden to them. I should* [marry] *and be a bad*
> *wife, and have a lover and make my husband's life wretched.*

"Please don't think I have the least desire to be married,"
Louise announced petulantly, "because I haven't." Given the
emotional climate of the Scott Russell family over the past
five years, it is not surprising that *one* of the sisters should
have been put off marriage permanently.

Louise's attitude, however, had quite the opposite effect
upon Alice. Her new fiancé, Baxter, had been living and
working in Paris. He had been in England for the holidays
and was about to return to France. Alice promised she
would wait a year for him and marry him the following
Christmas. Baxter left the country. Alice bade him a fond
farewell and promptly forgot about him! She must have
known that she would never be able to sit still in Sydenham
for a whole year, and so shortly after Baxter's departure,
she began to see Frank Rausch (Rachel's former admirer),
who was *still* very much in the picture. In a month Alice
decided she would marry him!

The changes of romantic commitment within the Scott
Russell family were taking place at a breath-taking pace,
and between Louise's decision never to marry, and Alice's

partiality for being engaged, one had to accord Mrs Scott
Russell a certain amount of sympathy — especially now,
for Rachel was about to return.

*Oh! Arthur how can I go home? Here a note of the music
we have heard together makes me cry. How can I ever
live in the old places full of dead memories and ghosts
of departed hope, with the knowledge of that loneliness.*

It was one thing to be without Sullivan in Switzerland,
but it would be quite another to be without him in Sydenham. "You are where I dread to go," she wrote him as she
was preparing to return. "You are where every place is full
of memories of our happy past — where every note of music
must bring some recollection of those glorious sunny days."

*My darling, why do you not write to me a few of the old
tender words with which I lived for so many years — to
help me in my utter loneliness — Arthur, Arthur, I have
torn out my heart and sent it back to you — but I quiver
from head to foot in every fibre with the pain. It is no use,
no words or deeds can change the fact or the love — and I
say to myself when I feel so desolate — you know he still
loves you with his great love. From morning till night I
work and never think, never dare think of the past or the
future — but at night — at night I always dream of you and
that you are with me and wake with the tears streaming.*

*And you — is it the same with you — yes — only you are
where I dread to go — you are where every place is full of
memories of our happy past — where every note of music
must bring you some recollection of those glorious sunny
days. Oh my God how we have paid for every hour —
every moment of happiness — and yet I would not undo
one of those six years — it is all I have left — Take me
mother earth. I have loved and been beloved . . .*

*I did not mean to write to you like this, but I cannot
help it — why should I put a veil between us — you know
every cranny and crevice of my heart and nature. Why
should I let you think I am calm and contented when I*

am what this letter shows you? And then I must have a few lines to help me — write to me just a few words — tell me how you are — if you suffer as I do — write to me to help me . . .
   — No, don't write, I could not bear it.
       The Lord gave and Lord Taketh away.
       Blessed be the name of the Lord.

After her return to Sydenham Rachel wrote several more letters to Sullivan in a similar vein. She just could not let him go, and Sullivan realized that he was going to have to 'end' the relationship all over again. He now found himself employing the same technique that Freddie Clay had used with Alice. Sullivan sent a letter to a third party — in this case George Grove — and in it he stated that work filled out his life at the moment and that, while he might marry one day, he had no intention of doing so at present. Grove, no doubt as intended, showed the letter to the ever-hopeful Rachel, who wrote Sullivan one more letter, dated almost exactly two years from the day upon which their affair had begun.

Friday, June 4, 1869

G. has just sent me your letter to him. It was cruel pain — but it was kind of him to show it to me — nothing <u>but</u> that would have convinced me that your love was changed. The tears come welling up from the agony even as I write — but God helps us all, we were put here to suffer — and it has all got to be borne and lived through — I shall be glad when the pain is over that your work fills out your life as it does. I suppose if I were a man it would be the same with me — but women's lives are so hard — so much harder than men's . . .

I suppose you will marry some day — as you say — and be celebrated and happy — you see, I was such a fool — I let everything go — and I have lost my health and my strength and my spirits and my love of life and <u>everything</u> — and I suppose my heart is broken — I do not know what else it can be.

Even now quivering with the pain I scarcely believe it is true — 6 long years — the love of 6 whole years — that it should die like that.

Forgive me for having bothered you — but you see I believed so in you — believed that any words were better than silence — judging by what I should have felt myself.

I was coming to see you in spite of everything — just to see if you still loved me. Oh! why did you take all my strength and the best years of my bright young life only to throw them away at the end.

Do you think if you had asked me to write a line to you to help you that I should have refused because of the pain it gave myself.

God bless you — Do you think if I come and put my arms round your neck and kissed you — you would push me away as if your love was changed. Oh! Is it all gone?

When you read this think of my coming to meet you 6 years ago in my blue cotton dress with the broad-brimmed hat.

Somebody has pulled the poor little passion flower and thrown it on the ground.

This time Rachel knew that it was over.

That summer of 1869, Sullivan wrote his first oratorio, *The Prodigal Son*, for the Worcester Festival. He had received the commission as a result of the success of his symphonic works of 1866 and 1867, the years of Rachel's greatest influence. "The book of *The Prodigal* is too beautiful," Rachel wrote, "and it made me weep to read it."

Sullivan wrote to Rachel occasionally that summer but he saw her seldom. Rachel was permitted to see the music when it was finished and to assist in the preparation of the final score. "I rejoice to do the copying," she told Sullivan, "and I want you to conduct from my copy — will you?" Rachel did not hear the oratorio at Worcester. It was the first première of a Sullivan work that she did not attend.

The Prodigal Son was a great success at Worcester. *Love Not the World*, the contralto solo, became successful as a separate ballad. The oratorio was Sullivan's first major vocal work. "I *glory* to think that you *could* not have written this before I knew you," Rachel wrote, still deluding herself.

I am far prouder of The Prodigal *than of anything because no man whose soul was not pure and noble could have conceived or executed such music.*

Sullivan's star had begun to rise, as Rachel had long ago dreamed it would. But his success would be the only part of Rachel's shattered dream that would be fulfilled. The fondest part of her dream, that she would influence his career and share his success with him, would never be.

All was not gloom in Sydenham, however, for three weeks after the Worcester Festival, Alice was planning to be married to Frank Rausch and the Scott Russell family was bristling with restrained excitement. Rachel, of course, was unhappy at the thought that Alice could be in love again so soon.

I am inclined to wish weddings had never been invented — at least other people's weddings.

—————◆—————

I am sad at heart — it seems so hard, all these wedding preparations and rejoicings and all because he is rich and associates with Dukes and Lords. It is a poor and inexcusable thing to my thinking — and I often feel bitter. "Love not the world" — people sing and say and feel — but do not act that.

In spite of Rachel's bitterness, Alice and Frank had a very happy engagement. Unfortunately they could not have had the happiest of weddings, with Alice's two elder sisters still in tears over Arthur Sullivan. Furthermore, the very fact that it was the *youngest* daughter who was marrying first was a signal to all of Sydenham that something was amiss within the Scott Russell household.

"Mr. Mahaffy performed the service very well," Louise wrote. "I may say he stopped a goodly time at 'If any person here present . . . ' and Mama and I suffered agonies." And well they might, for there *was* someone present at the wedding who would have had very good reason to object to it, and it wasn't Freddie Clay. At the last minute Baxter had returned from Paris! No-one had bothered to inform him that Alice had dropped him. He did not stop the ceremony, but he certainly shook everbody up.

After the wedding Louise wrote:

Mr. Rausch is by far the nicest man she has ever known, so good, such a sweet nature and so very lovable and if she is not perfectly happy it will be her fault.

Rachel's characteristic description ran:

They are a very nice couple, but it is not <u>ideal</u> love at all — not a thing which would cling if everything else failed — at least I do not feel that, or as if there were anything "holy" about it, do you?

In Rachel's state of mind, of course, no-one whom Alice had married would have been acceptable — least of all someone whom she herself had rejected. Nevertheless, Alice's 'compromise' marriage lasted well into the twentieth century, some twenty-five years after Rachel's death. So much for ideal love.

During the week of Alice's wedding, Rachel's former suitor, Harry Wynne, announced his engagement to Miss Goold, a young Irish girl that Louise had introduced him to. (Louise was still seeing to everybody's love life but her own.) Rachel's friends were marrying one after the other. Harry Wynne's engagement was further proof that one did not have to marry the *first* person with whom one fell in love, but this held very little meaning for Rachel.

As the autumn wore on Rachel found herself making a few more attempts to see Sullivan, but he steadfastly refused to meet her. Finally, Rachel decided that all romance had gone out of her life and that she had no choice but to leave Sydenham. Her brother, Norman, was the manager of Messrs. Baird & Co., an English shipbuilding and engineering firm in St. Petersburg. She would join him there. She booked a passage in the first week in January 1870. Before her departure she wrote to Sullivan once more.

I am so <u>cold</u> so <u>starved</u> for love . . . The beginning of winter is always sad and it brings back to me those bright days when you came in the afternoons and we sat round the fire and we had tea and chatted such nonsense.

Later she wrote:

I am coming to spend the afternoon with you on Friday to burn my letters.

Sullivan agreed to see her and he treated her with compassion. He told her that she must forget about the past. He told her that she must begin life anew in Russia; and he told her that she must, above all, try to bring a bit of joy back into her life, instead of stubbornly refusing all things which might make her happy. Rachel said that she would try, but she would probably have said anything at that moment if she thought that it might have pleased Sullivan.

He told her that he did not want to burn the letters she had sent him, and Rachel permitted him to keep them. Perhaps it was some comfort to her that Sullivan wanted to preserve at least the memory of their relationship, if not the relationship itself. Rachel too saved the letters which Sullivan had sent her and took some of them with her to Russia.

She left England just after the New Year and travelled via Berlin. Shortly after her arrival in St. Petersburg she wrote to Sullivan, *"Loyale je serai toujours, jusqu'à la morte."*

Louise also was far from free of Sullivan as she began to face the difficult winter of 1870. The new year was again presenting a major decision for the beleaguered Scott Russells. Their finances were still depleted though recently Papa's engineering talents had been more appreciated on the Continent. Once again the family began to consider moving abroad, and in March Louise wrote:

Papa's business is to be settled today so I suppose he will come home and soon, therefore, we shall leave Westwood. Dear Westwood to which we came 18 years ago, rich, prosperous, full of life and joy. We leave it poor and in adversity, leaving half our lives with much joy and sorrow there to begin a new life. Shall we serrer les lieus a little before we part or shall we gently let them loosen and break.

Life at Westwood was now far from what it had once been. The many days in which three once happy daughters had played the piano and sung until all hours of the morning with two brilliant composers, the days when the evenings rang with music were long gone. The house was a shadow of its former self. The family was sadly split up. Alice was married. Rachel and Norman were in St. Petersburg. Papa was away more than he was home, and Louise alone was left to look after Mama. "Fancy how lonely it is for her," she wrote to Sullivan that winter. "Don't be angry with me for not going on Thursday but I have made a rule never to leave Mamma more than once a week." Louise was still trying to maintain her own tenuous connection with Arthur Sullivan.

> *If I shrink from seeing you it is because you say you are hard and I cannot go through that pain again. It is like clinging to a marble pillar trying to get warm. It would at least be some gratification if the pillar would only say, "Do try and warm me," but no — it rejoices in its iciness.*

♦

> *Oh, if by loving you I could only make you well again . . .*

At the same time Louise was still encouraging Sullivan's relationship with Rachel.

> <u>Do</u> *Darling write to Russia. I am sure she longs for your letters. Why should you be hard? She loves you devotedly.*

Louise apparently never learned. Neither did she marry.

In the meantime Rachel was still thinking of Sullivan. "You are in my dreams every night now," she wrote, "and I am thankful that there should be some things that cannot die or alter or grow dim." Rachel was not making too many friends in Russia that winter. She preferred skating at night to a live band in the "illuminated garden". When the winter drew to a close she was quite ready to leave Russia, although she was far from ready to return to England.

> *I am going home in about four weeks but I hope only for a short time — and then to travel again. I could not stop quietly now — but feel a restless longing to move and change.*

Just before Rachel's return Sullivan invited *Louise* to dinner (ostensibly for his birthday). To her everlasting credit

Louise refused. In all probability, Rachel did not see Sullivan on that visit either. And after that there were no more letters.

A few weeks later Louise wrote to Sullivan annoucing the fact that Alice, married just a year ago, had had a baby.

Another destiny come to weave itself into ours.

During the next two years Rachel managed to recover somewhat from the damage that Sullivan had caused to her young life, but she was far from happy. The home she had grown up in and the friends that she had always loved only reminded her of things that were painful or past and dead.

Rachel had been an ambitious young girl. "Remember, I have staked my all on you," she wrote Sullivan during their engagement. "Win or fail?" she had asked philosophically of the future, "*first* or nothing, I answer," and apparently she believed what she had written. Without Sullivan beside her at the Crystal Palace, at the Groves and at the Glehns, the musical life of Sydenham afforded very little pleasure for her. She had returned home after her travels, but only, she hoped, for a short time. And so it turned out.

William Henn Holmes was one of the young men that Rachel had grown up with, and one of the few who was still unmarried. He was about a year or so younger than she was. Rachel had not seen him for some time, because he had been abroad. Holmes was a cousin of the Composer Charles Villiers Stanford, and was posted to Bengal in India.

Members of the Indian Civil Service used to return to England every few years on leave, and when they did they frequently found themselves wives in very short order. It was on one of these visits that William Holmes and Rachel met again. He called on her a few times. They began to enjoy each other's company, but they both knew that he would soon be going back to India. Would Rachel return with him?

In the eighteen months since she had last seen Sullivan, Rachel apparently had come to realize that if she were going to have any kind of a future at all, she would have to find some way of cutting herself off completely from the past. And so she did.

By the end of September, 1872, Rachel Scott Russell had burned Sullivan's letters and married William Holmes. Shortly after the wedding Rachel moved to India with her new husband, there to begin a new life, and to forget the past.

I stretch out my arms and feel I would give anything to feel the heat on my lips for one moment.

Rachel wrote that in the spring of 1869. And a short time later Louise wrote:

I have nothing more to give. Je suis épuisée ... at night some times I stretch out my arms into the empty darkness and feel as though my heart were breaking. I am so tired of life.

CHAPTER SIX

Epilogue

(1870 – 1900)

Whatever God ordained for us both, nothing can change the past — nothing — it is music — it has blended itself into our whole beings and will colour our lives to all eternity . . .
— Rachel to Sullivan

1, QUEEN'S MANSIONS,
VICTORIA STREET. S.W.

17. Nov: 1893

My dear Alice.

Are we really so old? not in feeling, believe you? Seems such a short time ago since we were playing about the house and garden at Westwood like children, and now — you maybe a grandmother shortly! and yet you are the youngest looking woman present of every age that I know, and I don't feel old.

having said this, I will now explain my delight that Ethel (Bertha?) is to be married, and my hope that she will be very happy, and be as good a woman as her mother.

I am going to Berlin (Bruno, and wish with all my heart that my proposed carried me to Scheffhausen instead), so that I might be the which myself and I left for all my free Sundays. Never know when the true thing is taken place, & send me a line to the Hôtel Bristol Unter den Linden, Berlin, (like a dear as I shall be there for the next ten days.

— Ever your affect
Arthur Sullivan

Sullivan had forced Rachel out of his life, but he could not force her out of his memory. He kept her letters all his life and never again shared so much of himself with another woman.

1872, the year that Rachel married, was the year in which Arthur Sullivan began to have serious kidney trouble. The pain attacked him mercilessly at irregular intervals for the rest of his life. Often the attacks would continue for many months. In the end they shortened his life by many years.

In March 1878 Louise Scott Russell died unexpectedly of consumption. She was thirty-seven years old. True to her resolve she had never married. The year in which she died, Sullivan suffered the worst kidney attack of his life and in July underwent crude surgery in Paris.

Sullivan saw Rachel once again at a party at John Millais' in the spring of 1881. They were obviously pleased to see each other, and they chatted together for several hours. But it was now more than ten years since their sad goodbye; Rachel was living a new life, and Sullivan was still living his old one.

In 1882, John Scott Russell, saddened by the break-up of his family, died at the age of 74 on the Isle of Wight. Life had not been kind to him. He had outlived his eldest daughter and saw another lose her happiness. His business had failed, and he wound up spending his final years, as he had many of his early years, in reduced circumstances.

In 1882, also, only six weeks after her father's death, Rachel Scott Russell, having given birth to two daughters, died unexpectedly in India at the age of thirty-six.

Sullivan did not share these tragedies with the Scott Russell family. In fact, after Louise's last letter in 1870 he fell out of touch with them almost completely until one afternoon in 1884 when a most unusual event occurred which called much of his past into review. On 30th April the entry in Sullivan's diary reads, *Mrs. Scott Russell came to tea*. He had not seen her for fourteen years.

Sullivan was forty-two years old. He had already written *HMS Pinafore, The Pirates of Penzance* and *Patience*. He had recently been knighted. He was the most successful composer in England. He had finally achieved all the prestige that

Sullivan's drawing room in Queen's Mansions — the room in which he probably served tea to Mrs Scott Russell. He had come a long way since Ponsonby Street

Rachel, Louise, Alice, Fred Clay, George Grove and the senior Scott Russells had talked and argued and dreamed about two decades before; and he and Mrs Scott Russell spoke of this in his magnificently appointed new flat in Queen's Mansions — the home which he would never ask a woman to share with him.

Sullivan's success would have pleased Rachel. She would of course have preferred symphonies to operettas, but she had had great musical insight and was aware of Sullivan's growing dependence upon a written text. She would have looked upon his partnership with W. S. Gilbert as an acceptable compromise with his Muse. Sullivan's musical inspiration had to come from *without*, and Rachel would have understood this.

But there were other things about Sullivan in the 1880s that would not have pleased Rachel: his gambling for instance, his partying, his club life, and of course his mistresses. Sullivan never married and he never allowed his mistresses to move in with him. He did not invite them to the parties that he gave at Queen's Mansions, and he never allowed these women to be seen with him in public. All through his life he would see his mistresses only privately — one might almost say in secret.

On that spring day in 1884, however, Mrs Scott Russell came to visit the man who had brought anything but happiness into the lives of two of her daughters so many years before. She and Sullivan probably passed a quiet afternoon. Knowing the composer in his middle years, he and Mama would have reminisced about the past, traded misfortunes, and then agreed to forgive and bear no grudges.

But if Sullivan had made any mistakes in his life, he would have been quite unaware of them on the day that "Mrs Scott Russell came to tea". The Savoy Theatre had recently opened, and he was just then feeling very comfortable. But Mrs Scott Russell would not have seen him that way. She had known him too long and too well to have been fooled by appearances. She knew how Sullivan made decisions, and how he tended to use what was given to him.

She would not have seen him as England's most prominent musician. She would have seen only the man who had chosen

The Pirates of Penzance over symphonies and concertos, and the man who had turned away from marriage. And Mama may also have known that the image of success and security which Sullivan was projecting that afternoon would not always be with him.

The next ten years would go by a great deal faster than the decade during which Sullivan first came to Sydenham, began to make his reputation, and met and turned away from Rachel Scott Russell.

The whirligig of achievement that filled Arthur Sullivan's middle years hardly afforded him the time to consider whether he was living the life that he wanted, and composing the music that he would have preferred. And there was nobody close enough to him to tell him that he was not.

It took a long time for Sullivan's lifestyle to catch up with him. He almost got away with a lifetime of partying and club life, of casual relationships and following the path of least resistance. But in his later years, failure and illness began to overtake him.

Sullivan had fifteen years of brilliant success with W. S. Gilbert. Then he quarrelled with him, separated from him, and found himself unable to achieve success on his own. In his declining years he had the misfortune to witness the organization of the Savoy Theatre, which he and Gilbert had helped to build, crumble before his eyes.

As the 90s wore on, failure followed hard upon failure for Sullivan, and one period of painful incapacity followed another. He had to live through much illness in his final years, and endure it alone. He found himself spending less and less time in London at the end, and more and more on the Continent, away from his friends, away from his work, in a seemingly endless pilgrimage from grand hotel to hotel. He had had his success. He had made his fortune, yet how different it was from the dreams on the lawns at Westwood thirty years before; how different from the life that Rachel had planned for him.

(Opposite) Arthur Sullivan shortly before his death, prematurely aged through years of illness

Though we are not near, still, darling, in spirit we are close together. Nothing can separate our souls now. Still in the darkness we can feel the other's hand guiding, helping onwards.

———◆———

I want you to live so that at any moment if your father's voice called up to you from the sky and you looking up saw his dear face, you could meet his eyes boldly and bravely and say, Father, I am leading the life you would have me lead . . . Good-bye for a little while.

AUTOBIOGRAPHY

OF

HECTOR BERLIOZ,

MEMBER OF THE INSTITUTE OF FRANCE,

FROM 1803 TO 1865.

COMPRISING

HIS TRAVELS IN ITALY, GERMANY, RUSSIA, AND ENGLAND.

TRANSLATED BY

RACHEL (SCOTT RUSSELL) HOLMES,

AND

ELEANOR HOLMES.

IN TWO VOLUMES.

VOL. I.

LONDON:

MACMILLAN AND CO.

1884.

First English edition of the memoirs of Hector Berlioz. After Rachel moved to India she continued her interest in music. This translation, her only major published work, was printed in England two years after her death. (British Library)

An envelope addressed by Rachel, showing one of the postmarks

NOTES

128

BIBLIOGRAPHY

Most books that have been written about Sullivan are inaccurate or incomplete in the portrayal of his life in the 1860s. The following, however, have been useful in providing information on Sullivan's early years or life in Sydenham.

Allen, Reginald, *Sir Arthur Sullivan, Composer and Personage*, New York, 1975.

Beaver, Patrick, *The Crystal Palace*, London, 1970.

Emmerson, George S., *John Scott Russell*, London, 1977.

Foster, Myles Birket, *The History of the Philharmonic Society of London, 1813–1912*, London, 1912.

Graves, Charles L., *The Life and Letters of Sir George Grove, CB*, London, 1903.

Grove's Dictionary of Music and Musicians, J. A. Fuller-Maitland, Ed., London, 1910.

Lehmann, R. C., *Memories of Half a Century*, London, 1908.

Millais, John Guille, *The Life and Letters of Sir John Everett Millais*, London, 1898.

Musical Times, The, London, 1862–1870.

Musical World, London, 1862–1870.

Olsen, Donald J., *The Growth of Victorian London*, Batsford, 1976.

Rogers, Clara Kathleen Barnett, *Memories of a Musical Career*, Boston, 1919.

Wyndham, H. Saxe, *Arthur Seymour Sullivan*, New York, 1926.